The Golden Therapy

Cognitive Behavioural Therapy & Hypnotherapy

Sharlene Sema Raston

TABLE OF CONTENTS

Biography

I, Sharlene Raston, author of the book "On the Road to Enlightenment – A philosophical way of looking at things" and "The Secret Letters of a Psychotherapist" was born in Harare, Zimbabwe and soon after I moved to Maputo, Mozambique. I studied at the Portuguese school in Maputo, and in 2004 I moved to Pretoria, South Africa.

I am a Life Coach and NLP Practitioner, I follow the Cognitive Behavioural Therapy approach on Psychotherapy and Hypnotherapy and have been registered in Psychometry (PMT 0086835) with the Health Professions Council of South Africa since 2011.

I completed my Honours Degree in Psychology at the University of South Africa (UNISA) and my Bachelor's degree at the University of Pretoria where I specialized in Psychology and Criminology. I completed a Diploma in the various Treatments and Effects of Addictions at the Open College University in the United Kingdom, I did my Life Coach and NLP Certificate through School of Life (South Africa) and own a certificate in Basic principles for First Line Managers from UNISA, SA.

My Psychometric training was carried out through UNISA; I gained a vast amount of knowledge while working in South Africa and got accreditations for the Personal Profile Analysis tool (PPA) at Thomas International,

Cognitive Process Profile tool (CPP) at Cognadev and the Learning Potential Computerised Adapt (LPCAT) developed by Marie De Beer.

I have many years of experience in the corporate world in Management in the Telecommunications Industry and Psychometric Testing. In 2016, I went to London to undergo training in Cognitive Behavioural Hypnotherapy at the UK College of Hypnosis and Hypnotherapy, one of the world's leading accredited hypnotherapy schools specializing in an evidence-based approach. I had also trained in Rational Emotive Behavioural Therapy (REBT) at the CCBT College in London, which is a pioneering form of Cognitive Behavioural Therapy (CBT) developed by Albert Ellis. For my Continuous Learning Development, I had the privilege to attend some seminars from Windy Dryden who is one of the leading practitioners and trainers in the UK in CBT and the first Briton to be accredited in REBT at the Albert Ellis Institute. The fundamental notion about REBT is that it is not the events that happen in our lives that disturb us, but the belief that we hold about the events that disturbs us, in other words, we disturb ourselves.

In 2019, I got certified as a Life Coach and NLP practitioner at School of Life in South Africa.

I have combined the knowledge and training I had acquired over the years from the great philosophical thinkers into developing my unique view and perspective.

I wholeheartedly love what I do. I truly love and value working with people and recognize the priviledge of being part of their journey. I see a side of them that is so real, true, raw, and human. In society, everybody is too busy acting like the most influential human being on earth, cold, putting on a mask to chase success — trying to hide their emotions so as not be perceived as weak. It gets to a point that we can no longer know someone for real, due to the mask everyone constantly wears. In the therapy room the mask falls off completely, and I see people's real selves. I manage to see a human being in front of me, and I love it.

My passion for philosophy has been alive from the moment I was exposed to it at the school where I was known as Descartes. Moreover, I am now continuing the chosen path of being a writer.

Introduction

Cognitive Behavioural Therapy known as "the Golden Therapy" is the umbrella term for a group of therapies such as Cognitive Processing Therapy (CPT), Cognitive Therapy (CT), Dialectical Behaviour Therapy (DBT) and Rational Emotive Behaviour Therapy (REBT). It is a form of psychotherapy scientifically tested and found to be effective in a wide range of mental health problems such as: anxiety related conditions, panic attacks, depression, and eating disorders, sleeping problems, relationship problems, self-esteem issues, procrastination and many more.

My goal is teach you specific and necessary skills that you can use for the rest of your life and empower you to become your own therapist. These skills involve identifying distorted thinking, modifying beliefs and changing behaviours.

We believe that it is not the events in our lives that make us disturbed but how we perceive the events that lead to emotional disturbance. If we profoundly change our philosophy and thinking then we are more likely to profoundly change our feelings and behaviour.

In this book I will be placing greater focus and provide a critical view of Cognitive Therapy (CT) and Rational Emotive Behaviour Therapy (REBT) that shall allow you to develop expertise knowledge in this field of psychology and equally benefit from the specialized teachings.

I will be focusing on providing great knowledge and understanding on how to efficiently overcome conditions such as procrastination, anxiety, relationship difficulties and I will be sharing an in-depth understanding of the Cognitive Behavioural Hypnotherapy approach – evidence-based and address some of the most common myths surrounded the nature of hypnotherapy.

I will equally guide you into the process of living a meaningful life that allows you to feel fulfilled. You shall benefit from the secrets to experiencing life with colourful and wonderful lenses.

The greatest purpose of this book is to allow you to have access to privileged and expertise knowledge that is not easily available, with extremely high potential of changing your life and consequently those around you.

After reading this book, prepare yourself to never be the same again.

CHAPTER 1

Critical Evaluation of REBT and CT

Cognitive behaviour therapy has found to be an effective and preferred method by Mental Health Practitioners which focuses on guiding the client to a rational and healthier living, by the use of cognitive and behavioral methods proven to be effective in thousands of research papers conducted.

I will be focused on the critical evaluation of the REBT (Rational Emotive Therapy) theory developed by Ellis and the CT (Cognitive Theory) developed by Aaron Beck. The purpose is to evaluate the differences and similarities between the theories as well as the strengths and weaknesses of both theories.

CT (Cognitive Theory) is a form of therapy widely used to treat a variety of mental health problems, based on the idea that what we think influences how we feel and therefore it influences our behaviour. In other words our thoughts, feelings and behaviour are interconnected.

REBT focuses on resolving psychological disturbances by changing irrational beliefs to rational ones. It is perceived as a philosophical approach whereas CT has been gaining its wide recognition due to the vast amount of the empirical studies done on the field.

Both theories appear to be highly successful in helping clients to overcome psychological disturbances, there are a lot of similarities between them however there are fundamental differences that distinguish them and will be discussed throughout the chapter.

The chapter will focus on giving background information about each theory, an evaluation regarding the similarities of both theories, the key differences between both perspectives and lastly a conclusion in which the information is integrated.

I.   REBT Background

In 1955, Albert Ellis developed REBT as a form of cognitive behaviour therapy that believes that what we think about the events directly influences our emotions and behaviour. Ellis believes that the activating event contributes to how we feel or behave but it is our belief or philosophy that make us feel the way we do, which means that we disturb ourselves.

REBT is a practical, goal-oriented approach which focuses on the "hear and now", identifying unhealthy emotions, beliefs that cause a negative impact on the person's life and psychological disturbances. Ellis believes that the human beings in general hold assumptions about themselves and the world that may be rational or irrational, and these assumptions determine how we react to the different situations we are faced with. In addition to that, it provides a variety of methods to help the individual to reformulate their irrational beliefs to more rational and helpful ones by the use of a technique called "disputation". Most importantly, it helps the individual develop a new philosophy in life that will allow them to successfully use the learnt strategies in the different areas of their lives to avoid disturbing themselves.

Albert Ellis was not very impressed with psychoanalysis and instead was widely influenced by stoic philosophers, mostly Epictetus who stated that:

"Man is not disturbed by things but by the views he takes of them" (Epictetus).

II.   Cognitive Behavioural Therapy

In 1967, Beck developed CT (Cognitive Therapy), a present-oriented form of therapy, focused on problem solving and widely used to treat patients with depression.

He believes that the way we view the situation is more related to our reaction to the situation than the situation itself.

In this form of therapy, the therapist assists the clients in identifying their dysfunctional and unhelpful thoughts, challenge them and most importantly try to apply new views, and alternative ways of perceiving the situations in order to improve their mood and functioning.

Beck identified three mechanisms that are widely responsible for depression which are (a) The cognitive triad (negative view of the self, world and future); (b) Negative self-schemas; (c) Errors in Logic (thinking distortions).

Research found that CT had a high success rate in treating patients suffering from depression and had a lower relapse rate compared to drug treatment based on the premise that depression has a cognitive basis (McLeod, 2008).

III.   Differences and Similarities of REBT and CT Therapies

According to Christine A. Padesky and Aaron T. Beck (2003), REBT and CT both developed in 1950s and at that time Ellis took on a philosophical basis whereas Beck had decided to focus on doing research on depression in order to get empirical evidence regarding depression. It appears that Beck focused greatly on the research component of its therapy and according to   Ellis (1980), CT does not put enough emphasis on the philosophical nature. Ellis perceives the philosophical component as significantly important as he holds the view that human beings are born philosophers who associate meaning to their experiences and his main focus is on making profound philosophical changes in them in order to have an effect on their future, emotions and behaviours. Ellis focuses on the human beings irrational beliefs as cause of their disturbances which are therefore created by themselves and if they can choose to disturb themselves this means that they can also undisturb themselves by changing their philosophy and thoughts, feelings and behaviour. On the other hand, Beck places more importance on the dysfunctionality of the beliefs as opposed to their irrationality and the therapist helps the client to evaluate the functionality of their beliefs based on their experience (Becks & Padesky, 2003).

Both theories help the client in changing their cognition however they use different methods in order to achieve it. Beck, uses Socratic dialogues, behavioural experiments, automatic thought records, psychodrama, and core belief logs and on the other hand Ellis uses the process of disputation (Becks & Padesky, 2003). The use of disputation techniques is done by disputing the clients irrational thinking as well as teaching the client to do their own disputation which Ellis argues that this process may be more efficient when dealing with young children, mentally retarded individuals or psychotic individuals who may not be suitable for Socratic-type dialogues and may be more efficient to simply teach them rational coping statements (Ellis, 1980).

Both therapies teach the clients distraction methods including progressive muscle relaxation to help the clients with worries and to promote behavioural change, however Ellis (1908), believes that it is important to focus on their philosophy because these methods promote temporary well-being as opposed to long-term well-being that may be achieved by focusing on managing their irrational beliefs.

Based on the Beck Institute organization, once the therapist identifies the client's dysfunctional thinking by asking questions such as: "What is going through your mind right now?" the therapist helps the client changing their inaccurate thinking to a more accurate one by helping them examine the validity and helpfulness of the thoughts. This approach differs greatly to Ellis's approach in which the therapist assumes what the client says to be true and makes the connection with the "musts" and "should" that constitute the irrational beliefs that the client holds. (Becks & Padesky, 2003). Ellis (1908) believes that this way he manages to focus on the emotional problem that he sees as the original difficulty as opposed to practically solving the problem, as he believes CT does.

The relationship between the client and the therapist is collaborative in both therapists but according to Ellis (1908), CT tends to be less selective than with his approach. Ellis focuses more on acceptance as opposed to giving warmth and approval to the client as he does not want the relationship to influence the client set of belief system where the client may think that the therapist thinks "they are good people" but to promote unconditional self-acceptance instead. Both therapies promote the homework assignments in between sessions, which will help them, incorporate what they have learnt in the sessions. Beck & Padesky (2003) see REBT as a less collaborate form of therapy because the therapist takes the role of an expert in the relationship as opposed to Becks that places more emphasis on the client discovering misconceptions for themselves and believe that REBT may be regarded as confrontational.

Dryden (2009) points out that A. Beck has developed a problem list in the treatment of depression to use with the clients to help them identify their emotions and in order to bring structure to the therapy. This method is used by both therapies in order to bring a sense of order during the therapy session.

With regards to the use of behavioural techniques during therapy, both therapies use different behavioural methods however Ellis (1908) is more selective on the procedures used and appears to show some reservations about operant conditioning even though it is used during therapy too. Ellis explains that due to his view on the importance of changing the philosophical view of the client and make the client more independent about social influences, individualistic and nonconformist he does not want the client to do the homework assignment due to the praise of the therapist for doing it, which would be equivalent to doing the right thing due to the wrong reasons.

Both theories favour in vivo desensitization, and Ellis (1908) tends to use it with more frequency through homework assignments in which he emphasizes the need for the client to face their unhelpful fears and to deal with low frustration tolerance, which has long-term consequences as the client learns to develop high frustration tolerance. This is reflected in the way Ellis describes the therapy as being "implosive" therapy in which the clients are encouraged to engage in their phobic behaviour suddenly and repetitively in order to face their irrational thoughts and ideas and consequently develop high frustration tolerance too, that they can't bear the situation.

Both therapies highlight the importance providing skill training to the client in the different areas of life, but according to Ellis (1908) the change of irrational beliefs is of utmost importance.

According to Padesky & Beck (2003) they differentiate CT by being empirically based and REBT to be philosophical based. Ellis (2005) disagrees with this and states that both theories are philosophically and empirically based. He mentions the fact that he worked with Psychoanalyses and the Carl Rogers system for a couple of years and he empirically found the methods to be unsuccessful and ineffective which led him to find more effective ways of treatment and he developed REBT.

IV.   Conclusion

In conclusion, both theories CT and REBT have a strong foundation in which it emphasizes the fact that it is not the situation that causes our feelings and emotions but our perception of the event that causes it. It could be argued that both theories agree that we ourselves cause our own psychological disturbances by our irrational thinking, or interpretation of the events as Ellis defends or by our dysfunctional thinking and distortions as Beck states which leads to the conclusion that both theories do have a philosophical basis.

The theories appear to be very similar in the importance given in our cognition and the therapist helps the client to manage it in a way that will lead the client to live a functional life with rational and helpful ways of looking at the world, themselves and others. And they place equally great importance in the behavioural aspect of the therapy too which is mostly used for homework assignments in between therapies as both therapies believe that it is ideal for the client to apply what he has learnt in therapy into the everyday life as it is fundamental for the process of change.

Both theories appear significantly unique, elegant and effective in the treatment of psychological disturbances.

References:

Albertellis.org. N.p., 2017. Web. 9 Mar. 2017.

"Beck Institute For Cognitive Behavior Therapy". *Beck Institute for Cognitive Behavior Therapy*. N.p., 2017. Web. 9 Mar. 2017.

"Cognitive Behavioral Therapy | CBT | Simply Psychology". *Simplypsychology.org*. N.p., 2017. Web. 9 Mar. 2017.

Dryden, Windy. *How To Think And Intervene Like An REBT Therapist*. 1st ed. Hoboken: Taylor & Francis, 2009. Print.

Ellis, Albert. "Discussion Of Christine A. Padesky And Aaron T. Beck, "Science And Philosophy: Comparison Of Cognitive Therapy And Rational Emotive Behavior Therapy"". *Journal of Cognitive Psychotherapy* 19.2 (2005): 181-185. Web.

Ellis, Albert. "Rational-Emotive Therapy And Cognitive Behavior Therapy: Similarities And Differences". *Cognitive Therapy and Research* 4.4 (1980): 325-340. Web.

Padesky, Christine A. and Aaron T. Beck. "Science And Philosophy: Comparison Of Cognitive Therapy And Rational Emotive Behavior Therapy". *Journal of Cognitive Psychotherapy* 17.3 (2003): 211-224. Web.

CHAPTER 2

Cognitive Behavioural Hypnotherapy

Cognitive Behavioural Hypnotherapy is an evidence-based approach which combines Cognitive Therapy and Behavioural Therapy by adding Hypnosis. Throughout this chapter I will be explaining this method in great detail the theoretical and practical knowledge of using this approach for treatment purposes.

Client suitability for Therapy

Hypnotherapy is one of the most effective forms of therapy, however it is very important that the therapist has enough knowledge to assess client suitability. In other words, there are clients who are more suitable for therapy as the effectiveness of the therapy depends on a number of factors. It is the work of the therapist to look at factors such as the severity of the symptoms, as the more severe the symptoms are there is evidence that predict poorer outcome, clients that show functional impairment, which is when the symptoms of impairment are present in different spheres of their lives or when the client shows signs of having a personality disorder. In addition to that, there are other factors that contribute directly in positive or poor outcome of the therapy such as the clients expectancies, whether the client has a positive perception and expectation of the results; client's readiness for change plays a significant role in the outcome of the therapy as if the client is still not ready it may lead to poor results; whether the client has positive personality traits that can assist the client in developing strengths to cope with the presented problems as well as psychological mindedness, a client that has an insight and is not able to have a good psychological understanding of his suffering may have more difficulty overcoming the problems. On the other hand, the behaviour of the client during the therapy plays a significant role in the outcome too. Research shows that clients that participate less during the process are less likely to benefit from therapy and evidence also shows that the lack of therapeutic alliance between the therapist and the client may also lead to poorer results. However, it is extremely important that the therapist keeps clear boundaries with the client and does not develop a friendship as this may have a negative impact on the outcome of the treatment.

There are times that the clients have unsuitable requests which are not fit for therapy, as an example, some clients may go for therapy with the aim of changing their husband's behaviour, unfortunately that is unsuitable as we as therapists can help the client deal with the situation in a healthier manner and in relation to a set goal, but we cannot change anyone else. Another example could be a client that goes for therapy because they would like to quit a substance such as alcohol for example, but not from free will but because they have pressure from a family member to quit. It is important that the client goes for therapy and shows readiness for change that comes from within as opposed to being forced upon to change. Lastly, some clients are interested in doing past life regression; even though there are some hypnotherapists that agree with doing it, in cognitive behavioural hypnotherapy it is not recommended to do it because there is no scientific evidence of the reliability of the memories, therefore we should not encourage clients to do past life regression.

The Initial Consultation with a client

The initial consultation is the most important session of the therapeutic process for various reasons and one of them is that it determines the relationship and therapeutic alliance the client and therapist will have. Therefore it is vital that the therapist brings a feeling of trust as well as confidence to the client as the client will also form an opinion based on the therapist behaviour. The initial consultation is when the therapist gathers all the relevant information from the client, such as basic information but also past information on whether the client has been for therapy before and the outcome of it, we assess the present issues, the impact, duration and coping mechanisms. The therapist assesses the client to see if there are any contraindications, in other words to see if the client is suitable for therapy, for example if a client suffers from a personality disorder such as schizophrenia it is an indication that he/she is not suitable for therapy. Therefore, having a health assessment questionnaire is equally important in order to measure health factors and suitability. Ideally a therapist would also use clinical questionnaires in order to measure if the client suffers from depression, anxiety or phobias and if yes, the severity of it, as that would also determine the suitability of the client. As a client with severe depression, as an example would not be suitable for therapy too. It is important that a client is within my sphere of competence as sometimes the best treatment to a client can be to refer to someone that falls within their sphere of competence. Get the client's GP contact and discussing with the client the issue of confidentiality.

On a different note, it is important to explain what hypnotherapy is, discuss expectations, any fears the client may have with regards to hypnotherapy, any questions and misconceptions to make sure that the client is clear on what the therapy involves and to avoid any type of disappointment. Lastly, the first session gives an opportunity for the therapist to build a rapport, look at modalities and discuss payment.

Based on my personal experience, I found that if I fill in the questionnaire for the client, it helps for both of us to get engaged in the session and I get more comprehensive information as opposed to the limited information I would have had if the client filled in on their own. On the other hand, that also helps in the therapeutic alliance as we both get engaged and connect. The more interest I show, the more I notice that the client gets more engaged and feels more comfortable speaking to me, and doing some active listening as well as bringing a sense of understanding also contributes for the therapeutic alliance. I noticed that the use of humour and empathy has a positive impact in the outcome. In addition to that, I found that following the order of a script is not necessary and the session benefits from flexibility as that too makes the sessions more meaningful and contributes greatly to the therapeutic alliance.

The role of rapport

One of the main obstacles of therapeutic progress has been identified as the lack of rapport between the therapist and the client. Albert Ellis has stated that when a client shows resistance to treatment it is simply a natural response to the therapist use of poor techniques. As I mentioned on the previous question, the first impression the client has regarding the therapist normally dictates the outcome of the therapy and the level of response to hypnotic suggestions, and therefore it is important that therapist is aware and takes a number of factors into consideration in order to fortify the relationship, to ensure trust and allow the communication to flow from both parts. This can be achieved by showing friendliness, being supportive, show unconditional positive regard, congruence, doing active listening, and showing empathy by allowing the client to feel understood and respected. Research has shown that some degree of self-disclosure within the boundaries, can benefit the therapy as it allows the client to perceive the therapist as a fallible human being too and it can fortify the connection. In addition to that, therapists are encouraged not to use leading questions that may lead the client to a certain interpretation of the events but to use open ended questions which allow the therapist to obtain more information, for example instead of asking: "How depressed do you feel today?" The therapist could ask: "How do you feel today?" On a different note, indirect questions also appear less intrusive and allows the client to be more reflective, for example, instead of telling the client: "Can you see that your thoughts have a direct influence to your feelings of anxiety?", therapist could ask, "If ten people were in the same situation you were, were they all going to respond in the same way you did?" and after the answer ask "Why? What would be different about others that make them respond differently?"

Based on the feedback of my therapy sessions I found that the clients enjoyed my friendliness, sense of humour, the use of open ended questions which allowed the clients to express themselves more, made them feel that I was interested in what they were saying and I also managed to make sure that it was done within boundaries as it is important that me as the therapist leads the therapy sessions and make sure that we don't get off topic. I noticed that building a relationship and connection with the client was the most important factor before initiating the session.

Ideally one would benefit from being more emotive while using hypnotherapy, make sure thatone is fully focused on the client by showing flexibility throughout the therapy session. Lastly, it is important to make sure that one uses an appropriate tone and volume why doing hypnotherapy and this can be achieved this by checking with the client right in the beginning if the tone is okay for them and if not, improve the tune.

The pros and cons of using different scales and tests to assess hypnotic responsiveness.

There are a number of scales that have been developed in order to measure hypnotic susceptibility, in other words they measure the degree of responsiveness to hypnotic suggestion by the client. The most widely used scale and viewed as the most important is the Stanford Scales of Hypnotic Susceptibility (SSHS) which consists in a variety of tests, 12 in total and the client is measured and scored by the degree of responsiveness to each test. There are pros and cons for using different scales however the purpose of its use is to identify on whether higher response scores led to better outcome of treatment. One of the advantages of using the scales is that it gives the therapist an indication on which technique the client may be more responsive in treatment. As an example, if a client scores low on the Negative visual Hallucination it gives an indication that visual treatments are not recommended for the particular client as the client responds less to suggestions. But on the other hand, the therapist confidence plays a crucial role in determining the clients' response, as higher expectation of success leads to better outcome. The SSHS normally takes an hour or more to be administered and therefore it is very time consuming. As an alternative, the standard arm levitation test is less time consuming, takes less than ten minutes to administer and score and therefore both the therapist and client could benefit from using it.

When using the susceptibility tests the client gains confidence as he passes the tests and the more tests he passes the higher the likelihood that he will pass the following tests which in turn increases the client's expectations. An example of a good suggestibility test is the Chevreuls pendulum which the chances are higher that the client will respond positively and by praising the client it increases the chances of success for the following tests. The hand lowering test in which the therapist suggests that it's becoming heavier and heavier is a fantastic test to increase suggestibility or the arm rigid test in which suggestions are given that the arm is becoming very rigid and cannot bend. It is important to emphasize that the success of these tools depend highly on how emotive the therapist is, on the tone, confidence of the therapist combined with the trust the client has for the therapist and positive expectation towards the outcome of the suggestions.

How to facilitate clients' responsiveness to hypnotic suggestion in the future?

Response to hypnotic suggestions differ from person to person, some people are highly responsive and others are less responsive, however research shows that most people are moderately hypnotizable. However, it has been shown that if the subject is less responsive to hypnotic suggestions the subject may benefit from hypnotic training. The subject shall be trained to have a thoroughly understanding about hypnosis, understand that through active and conscious participation to suggestions as well as positive attitude and expectations the subject may certainly develop the necessarily skills to benefit from hypnosis. The therapist during the different exercises used with the client to increase susceptibility, may suggest that the client is in full control, if he does not want something to happen it will not happen, however if he wants it to happen it will happen, and repeat the exercises until the client becomes aware that he is in control of his mind and he can respond to suggestions if he wants to, but his willingness is of high importance and therefore it is a collaborative exercise. In addition to that, the therapist shall help the client develop certain skills that may improve responsiveness. The Golden hypnotic skills training is a widely used one and it helps the client develop important skills to improve hypnotic susceptibility.

Focusing, which entails being fully focused on the suggested stimuli as opposed to let the mind get distracted by ideas entering it, and because our mind is always busy and intrusive thoughts always pop in our minds we teach them the thought-stopping technique, which is to imagine shouting "STOP" as soon as that happens or imagine the "STOP" sign for more visual individuals and return back to the initial thought. Another great skill is the letting go technique, which is a mindfulness-based CBT and Buddhist meditation practice, in which the thought comes in our mind, we observe the thought, and simply let go and go back to the previous intend thought.

We can imagine putting the thought on a leave and putting it on the river and let the thought go with the current on the river. These skills can be acquired through practice, therefore the client may benefit from them if we start every session with a short exercise in which they practice these skills. Other suggestion test that can be used after that are the hand heaviness, the hand levitation, Chevreul's pendulum and Arm catalepsy. It is important that the client feels relaxed and does not feel under any pressure to respond positively in all exercises, and that some positive responses praising also plays a significant role in improving the positive outcome of the exercises.

Roles and responsibilities of therapist and client in successful hypnotherapy

Successful outcome of therapy can be regarded as teamwork in which not only the therapist has roles and responsibilities but the therapy is equally dependent on the client's engagement in the therapy as active participants. In other words, the therapist uses his knowledge and techniques to guide the client, and walk with the client and not for the client. Some clients believe that going for therapy is enough for them to see change, however it is the responsibility of the therapist to explain how the therapy process works, remove any misconceptions the client may have with regards to hypnotherapy such as fears and unrealistic expectations. The therapist shall help the client develop realistic expectations regarding the therapeutic process as opposed to looking at it as a quick magical fix. For best results, the therapist should be aware of what techniques he is most comfortable and efficient using as well as the techniques that work best for the client and this knowledge can be obtained by asking the client regarding past experiences and what had worked better for them in the past in terms of therapy, self-help books, meditation, spiritual practices to mention a few.

It is the responsibility of the therapist to empower the client by making them understand and internalize the idea that they are capable of developing new skills with the therapist guidance and therefore make the client take ownership of their share of the therapeutic work.

As a therapist, I shall explain to them in clear words and in a straightforward manner his responsibilities. I would explain to them clearly the important of positive attitude to hypnosis as a strong contributor to the success of it, by perceiving hypnosis as useful, worthwhile, and see the benefits of it, the importance of positive motivation in which the client wants to be hypnotized and positive expectancy in which the client believes that he can be hypnotized and respond positively to the suggestions.

It is normal that clients sometimes simply have a sense of helplessness and can't see themselves changing, and therefore I would always make use of analogies. I would use an analogy that resonates with them best such as the driving analogy, and ask them questions such as: After you learnt all the theory on how to drive a car were you able to get in the car and drive it perfectly? What did it take for you to be able to drive and become an automatic process? On average, how many times did you have to drive until it became an automatic process? I would then relate their mastered skill with the therapy, that in order to master the skills it will require practice, dedication and time.

Lastly, I would also speak about their potential and capabilities and find evidence by asking questions about the different achievements in their lives, different skills and so forth, so they can see their potential. Therapeutic alliance will play a crucial role and I would need to make an environment conducive to trust and positive attitude.

Ethics

The General Hypnotherapy Register (GHR) code of ethics appears to be a very comprehensive, straight-forward, and holistic document which covers the ethics on different spheres. From my observation it is of high relevance to the hypnotherapy field but not exclusively. The document gave me a clear indication on the importance of transparency I should have with my clients, importance of working within my sphere of competence, the importance of making sure that absolutely no harm can be done to the client even if it means that I shall terminate the sessions as the client's wellbeing is of utmost importance. The clauses that I found more interesting are:

a) "Provide service to clients solely in those areas in which they are competent to do so and for which they carry relevant professional indemnity insurance."

This clause is one of the most important clauses at it is there to protect the client and make sure that I fully understand my sphere of competence and are able to work accordingly.

A successful therapist is a therapist that chooses the right clients. This does not mean that I cannot work with a problem that I haven't worked before but simply means that I should work with problems of which I have received appropriate training for it and have enough knowledge and skills on the subject. An example of a problem in which I do not have the training to work with is Schizophrenia. It is a very sensitive disorder and therefore it would be unethical for me to take a patient that suffers from the disorder and claim that I can help the client as there is a probability of causing psychological harm, I am not trained to do so and I would be deceiving myself and the client.

b) "Remain aware of their own limitations and wherever appropriate be prepared to refer a client to another practitioner who might be expected to offer suitable treatment."

This clause also refers to my sphere of competence and the importance of being aware of my limitations and to feel comfortable and confident referring the client if I see that I am not fully equipped in the subject. It is important to note that hypnotherapists to not diagnose, however there are assessments standard assessments that we use such as the GAD (Generalized Anxiety Disorder) in order to measure the levels of anxiety or the PHQ-9 (Depression Test Questionnaire) which measures the levels of depression and we can have an indication with regards to the severity of the condition.

I had a client who I detected that she was suffering from severe depression, after the second consultation I had a clear conversation with her that unfortunately it does not fall under my sphere of competence nor have I received any training for severe depression. I referred her to clinical psychologist who I believe will be more equipped to work with her. In addition to that, I told her that once she receives the appropriate treatment and she is CBT ready (ready for change), she is more than welcome to get back to me and we will happily continue the work with her.

c) "Use due care and diligence to avoid the implantation of false memories in the client and ensure that the client is made fully aware that memories experienced while in a suggestible state are not necessarily correlated with, or to be taken as, real and valid memories of either the client's past or actual events."

This is a very important aspect because of the misconceptions people have with regards to hypnotherapy and also because they tend to believe that their memories are 100% accurate and which would apply in hypnotherapy. Many people tend to request past-life regression or even regression to when they were younger and they believe in the memory constructs. It is important to make it clear to them that our memory is not 100% accurate and it is very creative indeed. It is important to explain to them that there is no scientific evidence which confirms that past-life regression is accurate and due to the fact that the cognitive behavioural hypnotherapy is evidence-based we do not do past-life regression as we work with findings and methods that have proven to be reliable, valid and free of bias.

Conditions that fall under a hypnotherapist sphere of competence

One of the most important things to take into account when working as a Hypnotherapist is ethical behaviour which includes working within the sphere of competence. Hypnotherapy can be used to treat a variety of conditions such as:

a) Stress and anxiety, which include social anxiety, different type of phobias, work-related stress, panic attacks, different types of fears such as fear of flying, fear of heights, and lack of confidence among others.

b) Habits, when it comes to habits it could be conditions such as nail-biting, licking the lips, and it also includes mild addictions such as smoking, binge eating but he must keep in mind that he cannot make changes to a clients' diet, nor advise the client to discontinue medication nor prescribe medications; these roles should remain exclusively to specialists in the area, unless the hypnotherapist is qualified to do so.

c) Depression has been a controversial topic because it is an ambiguous condition and it can easily be related to suicide thoughts, self-mutilation and psychotic symptoms of which hypnotherapy may be a contra-indication. In these cases it is important that the hypnotherapist gets hold of the clients' GP to ensure that he can safely use hypnotherapy to the client. Based on the seriousness of depression I would not recommend a treatment with a hypnotherapist only if the therapist is qualified to do so.

d) Hypnotherapy can be of benefit to those who experience anxiety towards public speaking, study skills, performance in different areas to mention a few.

There are other conditions that may be treated by a hypnotherapist but only if the therapist has is a qualified medical practitioner. The therapist in this case would be able to evaluate on whether hypnotherapy could benefit the client and whether it is suitable for the client:

1) Pain Management, which include back pain, chronic pain, pain due to surgery and so forth.

2) Relationship problems, the therapist may only work with couples, group dynamics if he had been trained to so.

3) Psycho-somatic conditions, which refer to conditions that are directly related to psychogenic factors, which include stress-related conditions such as Irritable Bowel Syndrome (IBS), skin conditions such as eczemas, warts, losing patches of hair on the head caused by stress to mention a few.

The above three conditions do not fall under the basic spheres of competence however if the hypnotherapist has had training and is qualified he may work with the client. If the hypnotherapist has a clinical psychology background he is free to work with clients who suffer from severe depression as an example as he is he has the required qualification to do so.

Reflective Practice and Evaluation of the Therapy Sessions

Reflective practice is an overall evaluation of the therapy sessions with the aim to be consciously aware of my behaviour, and the clients' experience, if the sessions met my expectations, being able to examine the rationale used to make decisions, examine my thoughts, emotions and cognitions and to evaluate the responses from the clients' side. Reflective practice can be done with a supervisor, with peers or on my own.

My reflective practice is normally done on my own, in which I make a comprehensive understanding and evaluation of the therapy session, I would look at my notes that I made during therapy, recap and think of different ways to improve. I may at times consult with other professionals on the field to hear their feedback while protecting the identity of the client. Another factor that helps tremendously is to ask the client to provide me with feedback and ways I can improve to increase the outcome of the therapy.

I would prefer to use the Gibbs reflective style and I follow the following steps:

1. *What happened?*

    At the start of my career I was doing some volunteer work and had a client who requested me to provide her with psychotherapy as she believed that she was going through severe depression for many years and she will go for therapy as a last resource, however she wanted to dwell in the past, and justify everything with past experiences. She was showing high resistance to change, she had a negative attitude about the outcome of the therapy, she was stubborn in all aspects and adamant that she will not change.

2. *What was I thinking?*

Listening to her complaining about being in a low mood, but without any drive to improve her life, nor take any action started to make me feel very frustrated with her. I thought that she is in love with her depression, she does not want to change and she is wasting my time.

3. *What was good and bad about the experience?*

The negative side about my experience is that her stubbornness did create frustration within me but on the positive note, even though I felt annoyed with her I did not show it.

4. *What sense can I make out of the situation?*

I found that is important that I make an effective selection of my clients and not simply take any client that does not fall under my basic sphere of competence, as it results in frustration for both the client and the therapist.

As the saying goes: "Do not teach a pig how to sing, it wastes your time and it annoys the pig". In addition that, the most ideal clients for my style of therapy are goal oriented clients.

5. *What else could I have done?*

    The client could have benefited more if I would show more empathy by letting her express herself and if I focused on making her feel understood and unconditional positive regard. Only after developing the trust, and rapport I could move to a treatment plan.

6. *What else could I have done?*

    The client could have benefit more from sarcastic questions as opposed to didactic which would allow her to find the answers herself.

7. *If it rose again what would I do?*

    In future I will make sure that the client understands fully what Cognitive Behavioural Therapy and hypnotherapy is, I would make clear and agree with the client their roles and responsibilities, I would make sure that I understand clearly the clients expectations and if I am the suitable therapist to work with them. In other words I would make sure that the process is clear and encourage the client to ask questions.

Clinical Supervision and Professional Obligations

Clinical supervision is one of the basic requirements for practitioners in different areas such as psychologists, counsellors and hypnotherapists. The main objective is to ensure professional development, facilitate learning from the experiences, receive some form of guidance in dealing with critical issues and above all else make sure that the client will benefit from a professional and good service.

During the supervision sessions the confidentiality factor plays a significant role and supervision provides an opportunity for the therapist to provide a better service for the client as well as increase the positive experience for the client. In the same way that the therapist does not tell the client what to do, and helps the client instead to find the answers for themselves, the supervisor likewise does the same with the supervisee.

There are different types of supervision that can take place and the most commonly used are:

(1) differential supervision which refers to the one on one supervision (with a supervisor more experienced than the supervisee) or (2) peer support group.

Supervision normally takes place once a month for 1 or 2 hours however the GHR requires that they have minimum 2 hours supervision every three months during the first 2 years of practice and after that the therapist is not required to continue but it is highly recommended that he maintains this arrangement. Another type of supervision can be done via telephone, skype or by email and it is important that the therapist keeps the records of it as they can be asked to provide evidence of the past year supervision at the time of the yearly registration. The GHR supports individuals that may need supervision whether it is one on one or peer group. Note that during supervision the client does not need to be identified therefore, the supervisee may benefit by using a code or initials in order to refer to the client

Supervision sessions that are done through skype, telephone or email may turn out a lot cheaper however it makes it more difficult for the supervisor and supervisee to develop rapport and therefore to maintain the relationship. With regards to group sessions, these are normally free of charge as it is an exchange of skills and it is beneficial for the entire group attending as gives more space for creativity, more knowledge and it will give the professionals the opportunity to share more ideas, learn from each other challenges and it facilitates a more supportive environment.

It is advisable that less experienced therapist's work with a more experienced and senior therapist in relation to them whereas more experienced therapists can benefit by working with a peer therapist. Working with a senior therapist is very advantageous as the supervisor can focus fully on the supervisee in strengthening his skills which leads to deeper learning however this form of supervision can be very expensive, mostly taking into consideration that the newly qualified therapist is probably not financially stable yet.

Supervision is interpreted by therapists in different ways, some have it simply because it is a requirement from the professional body but others truly see the benefit and value of it. Ideally all therapists whether they are experienced or not experienced shall benefit from it as learning and obstacles are never-ending.

Client confidentiality in Psychotherapy

Confidentiality is one of the main aspects of therapy, it is one of the most important issues to be discussed with the client before the beginning of therapy and the therapist should honour the commitment to keep all the information from the client whether it is shared, notes taken, exercises, personal information and tape recordings in a secure place.

It is fully the responsibility of therapist to maintain confidentiality under any circumstances unless otherwise required by law and therefore the exceptions to confidentiality should also be discussed by the therapist with the client to ensure that the client has a full understanding of its nature.

The circumstances in which confidentiality can be broken are normally if there is a court order that requires the therapist to disclose information, if there are issues concerning abuse/harm to self and others, if there is any risk concerning abuse of a child or if a child subject to maltreatment, if the client becomes suicidal, and if there are risks to the therapists or other therapist.

In addition to that, the therapist shall make sure that all records need to be kept in a secure place to make sure than no one will have access to it unless with authorization, if there will be anyone else accessing the client's information the client needs to be aware of it in the first session which also includes the supervisor, however even during supervision it is advisable to not use the client's name but rather use the initials or a code to refer to him. Based on the law, the client has the right to have access to his information or request from the therapist at any given time. On the other hand, if the client is a minor, the parents may request to have access to the information but this is a sensitive subject as in rare cases the sharing of information could be considered harmful to the health and safety of the client.

In cases of supervision, whether it is peer supervision, differential or another health or social care bodies, practitioners shall also maintain the confidentiality principle. However it is advisable that we consult the client before sharing the information in public for academic purposes such as research or workshops even though it is done anonymously.

Another aspects to take into account is that there is a probability that I may encounter a client outside the therapy sessions. Based on my policy and contract with the client I suggested that if we do see each other in public

I will not acknowledge the client specially if the client is accompanied by someone – so they don't have to explain who I am. Although, if the client shows openness to greet I will equally greet but shall keep the communication minimal as developing any kind of relationship with the client outside therapy may affect negatively the outcome of the therapy; if in the therapy waiting room there are more people and I shall call my client to the therapy room, I would prefer not to call his name but greet and directing him to the therapy room.

There may be cases that a husband or family member may call and say that because they are paying for the therapy they have the right to know details about the therapy – I am firm and shall not disclose any information

Psychotherapist duty of care and the role of informed consent in treatment

The two main laws which affect the practice of hypnotherapy are, informed consent and duty of care. These two are examples of common law however it is important to reiterate that these are not criminal offences. Common laws are laws that should be used by professionals, focus on his ethical behaviour and mainly protect the client by ensuring the therapist will choose the best treatment for the client and do his best to do no harm to the client in any given circumstance.

Informed consent is when the client with the best of his knowledge consents to any form of action such as a treatment and when he has full understanding on what the action entails, and any implications that may be related to it. It is the duty of the therapist to explain clearly what hypnosis is, explain the principles of the technique, get to a mutual agreement about it, clarify any questions the client may have, understand the client's expectations and make sure that it goes in line with the treatment and outcome of the treatment and explain the principles of the technique. Having all these factors tackled the client shall be in a better position to give informed consent as opposed to blind consent. When it comes to clients who are under 18 years old, it is important that the therapist gets the consent from the parents or guardian of the child.

Informed consent falls under "duty of care" which means that it is the therapist responsibility to make sure that the client had been provided with enough knowledge with regards to the therapy and that the expectation from the client and the outcome of the therapy are in line. In addition to that, the therapist is equally responsible for explaining to the client any risks or consequences that may arise as a result of therapy. As an example, a client that suffers from psychosis the hypnotherapist may not recommend hypnotherapy due to the unstable nature of the psychotic symptoms and to make sure that no harm can be done to the client that may be interpreted as a result of hypnosis. When faces with a client with certain medical conditions the therapist would benefit from discussing the treatment plan with the clients ' GP to ensure that it is a safe procedure to continue.

Lastly, there are no established laws related to hypnotherapy, there is only one law that is related to stage hypnosis. With regards to practicing as a hypnotherapist we will base on the general laws such us, working with the public, disability acts, children acts and data protection.

Risks associated with false memory syndrome and spontaneous or deliberate "abreaction" in hypnotherapy. How would you reduce those risks or managed their consequences.

In the early days, Freud popularized hypnosis and started using regression as a method in order to achieve therapeutic progress through personal insights. After using hypnoanalysis for approximately ten years he came to the conclusion that the method is not efficient and it has potential to cause harm to the patient in certain circumstances.

The use of regression in hypnotherapy has always been a subject of debate within the field as it arises many concerns with regards to safety and professional ethics. The major concerns about regression are abreaction and false-memory syndrome.

Abreaction is when past experiences which are normally fearful or related to strong emotions are evoked during the sessions and it is normally followed by therapeutic changes, however there are concerns because it may equally lead to re-traumatization.

In other words, making the client experience the past strong negative events in a vivid way may lead to Post Traumatic Stress Disorder. This can be developed right after the therapy or can be developed at a later stage, days or weeks later. Based on that, many psychologists perceives regression as one of the most potentially dangerous phenomena within the mental health profession.

Another factor that needs to be taken into consideration is that we do not know the nature of memory that the client will retrieve and nor the effect that it will have on the client. And if the memory is too strong and consequently makes the client feel distressed it is imperative to have a therapist who is trained and competent in order to calm the client down as by no means shall a therapist let the client leave the therapy while distressed.

If a therapist is faced with a distressed client during hypnosis the therapist can suggest that the client empties the mind, put the memory aside and can also use the "safe place" technique or help the client to focus on going deeper into hypnotic relaxation through suggestion and may also use images of emotional calm and stability. On the other hand, in order to reduce the risks of abreaction the therapist is advised to begin the therapy by using the ego-strengthening or confidence building technique to allow the client to become familiar with the process; the therapist may suggest to the client to only remember or relive experiences that he is able to deal with and lastly the therapist may agree with the client "bail-out" signals such as putting the left hand up and the therapist will slowly make the client go back to feeling relaxed and emerge from hypnosis.

When regression is used, the clients tend to experience very vivid memories of which they believe to be clear and accurate, however Freud had also identified that most of the time it is constructs from the brain, in other words the brain confabulates the memory but in fact these are False Memories. It is also very difficult to prove the veracity of the memories and therefore many psychologists have chosen to abandon the regression technique.

Cognitive-Behavioural hypnotherapy is evidence-based and therefore therapists are not advised to make use of these techniques due to the possible dangers involved and the inaccuracy of these memories.

A fictional client suffering from social anxiety: A multi-modal assessment of their symptoms and three sessions treatment plan

Peter works in the corporate environment as an operations manager and he had just been promoted to an executive positon of which he is expected to participate in high level meetings with the shareholders of the company in order to provide feedback of the company's performance, work on long-term strategies to increase revenue and discuss any present matters. Peter suffers from public speaking anxiety and as a result he starts blushing when he needs to speak during the meetings, his hands start sweating, his heart starts to beat very fast and as a result his voice shakes and it affects the clarity of his speech.

Due to his feelings of anxiety he avoids speaking during the meetings and only speaks when he has to. Peter seeks treatment to overcome his social anxiety and specifically in the work environment where it is more notorious as interferes with his performance at work.

In the first session I would focus on assessing Peter by using a multi-modal assessment of which I would assess his cognitions, behaviour and his feelings. I would opt for the Imagery-Based Recall script method in order to gather information, and this would give us an overview of the problem/situation, the behaviour, how the he responds in the situation, his coping skills and the consequences or feelings that he experiences. I would assign him a self-hypnosis CD for relaxation and ego strengthening.

In the second session, we would review the homework which refers to the self-hypnosis, ensure that we have gathered substantial amount of data with regards to his feelings, behaviour and emotions.

I would work with the ABC Exposure Therapy Script in order to work on establishing new beliefs. I would guide Peter into deep relaxation and establish the new beliefs repeatedly until the feeling of anxiety has reduced significantly. I would give him homework to continue doing self-hypnosis at home to increase his confidence levels. I would equally assign to Peter a low hierarchy behavioural assignment agreed between the two of us of which he exposes himself to the object of fear gradually within his capabilities.

On the third session we would review the homework task and discuss any challenges he faced as well as achievements. In this session I would use the Assertiveness & Authenticity script in order to allow him to develop his confidence, believe in himself and his potential and develop his assertiveness skills. I would assign the client a coping imager CD while working on his ego strengthening and we would agree on a higher hierarchy task as homework.

Role of hypnotic induction, deepening and emerging techniques; induction techniques and three deepening techniques used in hypnotherapy

It has been observed that clients tend to become more susceptible to hypnotherapy through habit and association of ideas. It is important that before starting the process the therapist makes sure to remove all misconceptions that the client may have with regards to hypnotherapy, make sure that the client has a realistic understanding of hypnotherapy, positive expectation and that he is emotionally reassured. The role of induction, is to increase suggestibility, expectation and motivation as well as take them to hypnosis which is a deeper state.

After the induction follows the deepening stage which is when the therapist helps the client intensify the hypnotic stage and he goes "deeper into hypnosis" in other words the client gets into a more intense relaxed stage by suggestions from the therapist such as "SLEEP DEEPER". Before the hypnosis come to an end, comes the process called emerging, which is the awakened stage. It is important that the emerging is done in a diligent manner and gradually. For example, the therapist may say to the client that "I am going to slowly count until 5 and as I say each number you start feeling more in touch with your senses and when I get to 5 you will be awakened and emerge from hypnosis."

It is important to use a simple technique that the client feels comfortable with, for example when using the eye fixation induction instead of using a pen, my finger can be more appropriate as some clients may feel uncomfortable with the pen, there must be a reasonable distance from the client to not appear invasive, some clients may not be comfortable if I touch them during the process and therefore it is important to ask them if they are comfortable with me touching them. Clients benefit from role modelling which can be done by showing the technique beforehand.

Example of inducing techniques are: the eye fixation technique I which I could use a pen, make the client fixate on the tip and I would slowly get the pen closer to his forehead by using suggestions that his eyes are getting more and more tired until they close.

The Analysis: Bernheim's induction method, the therapist suggest to the client that he looks at the therapist and is thinking of nothing but sleep and suggests that the eyes are getting heavier and heavier until the client sleeps.

The mothod I use the most is The Eye-Roll Induction technique, where the therapist suggests the client to look up towards the eyebrows as if there is a point in the middle of the forehead with the eyes closed and then to slowly open the eyelids looking up, roll the eyes up and back, take a deep breath, exhale slowly and close the eyes. After that, tell the client to sleep.

Examples of deepening techniques are, deepener by (1) Direct suggestions, where the therapist uses direct suggestions such as: SLEEP DEEPER; (2) Staircase deepener, where the client is suggested to visualize a staircase and gets deeper into hypnosis with each step; (3) Deepening by breathing, the client takes a deep breath and as the therapist suggests "SLEEP DEEPER" the client exhales and the feeling of relaxation intensifies.

The different range of techniques and strategies used to address different client presenting problems in hypnotherapy

Throughout the years, I have explored a variety of techniques and methods in order to address the client's problems through the use of hypnosis. The different types of induction techniques such as the eye fixation, making the client focus on a specific point and imagine that there is a very bright light and as they fixate the eyes start growing more and more tired until they are closed; as I explored different types of deepeners in order to address different types of issues and I equally saw the importance of the emerging techniques.

Each stage of the hypnosis is of equal importance and will determine the success of the therapy. It is of high importance that before using hypnosis that I discuss with the client regarding the misconceptions regarding hypnosis. I will highlight once again that it is important that he builds up trust towards me as the therapist, the environment needs to be conducive for the therapy session and the client needs to be comfortable. My clients benefited tremendously when I would familiarise them with the techniques by showing them how to do, also by explaining to them what hypnosis entails and the importance of collaboration and positive expectation for the outcome of the therapy. When using the different techniques it is important to pay attention and notice which techniques the client responds better to in order to focus on those and to be in touch with the client's experience. For example, if I suggest to the client to imagine a certain scenario and I continue by exploring the scenario it is important to check with the client if he is imagining it or if his imagination has shifted to something else to make sure that we are on the same page and increase the efficiency of the treatment.

Clients with negative and destructive thoughts may benefit from the Thought-Stopping protocol, this techniques is indeed one of my favourites and I use it very often. In order for the client to benefit from it is important that he develops mindfulness and self-awareness. This way if he is aware of his thoughts he can identify the trigger and straight away tell himself to STOP and use alternative thoughts instead that have been discussed in therapy and used during the hypnosis. Clients may also imagine a "stop" sign as they see the negative thoughts arising. It is important to familiarise the process with the client before using the method as some clients may not enjoy the therapy and may find slightly "aggressive" due to the tone used.

A client suffering from a phobia such as – spiders – could benefit from Desensitisation and coping rehearsal treatment, of which we would work with increasing the confidence and coping skills when faced in the situation. Through this technique I would be able to measure the client's progress, his coping skills and levels of anxiety.

Lastly, for a client suffering from unhealthy anger and would like to overcome his emotions I would use the ABC Exposure Therapy treatment, of which we would analyse the presenting problem, set the goal the client would like to achieve and use hypnosis in order to solidify and intensify the goals, the new suggested behaviour.

Self- hypnosis or autosuggestion techniques

Self-hypnosis is an important component during therapy not only for the client but for the therapist too. It is the role of the therapist to do hypnotic skills training experiments with the client and self-hypnosis. Therapists are also advised to use self-hypnosis techniques to themselves and most importantly in between sessions.

The main reason for that is to make sure that the tension from the previous session is not transferred onto the next session, in this case the therapist would benefit from relaxation self-hypnosis. In addition to that, one of the main goals of the therapist is to provide the client with a set of skills that will allow the client to become his own therapist and no longer depend on the therapist when faced with future situations and this can also be achieved by the use of self-hypnosis.

It is important to highlight that hypnosis refers to when the client responds to an idea, it can be described as focused attention by the use of imagination and focus on the response too.

The client is also trained to become aware of his thoughts as they pop up during the hypnosis, be able to detect involuntary thoughts and perceive the thoughts as spam as opposed to trying to fight the thoughts. The client is encouraged to be aware, simply let go of the thoughts and go back to the main focus. The more the client is exposed to hypnosis the higher is the probability to increase his hypnotic suggestibility and therefore assigned self-hypnosis is recommended to the client in between sessions.

Self-hypnosis is regarded as a powerful "convincer" and contributes to providing the client with the idea that he is a "good hypnotic subject", as a result the client is encouraged to perceive hypnosis as focused attention and expectation.

As a therapist I would opt to providing the client with an audio of which he can use for his self-hypnosis at the comfort of their home.

Examples of self-hypnosis that I could recommend are:

a) Relaxation stress-management which focuses on passive attention, the client learns to simply accept the ideas that may pop in his mind and learns to let go; incorporation where the client focuses on the internal and external sensations, deep breaths which allows deeper relaxation, followed by fractional muscle relaxation and passive breathing.

This exercise shall be used frequently in order to induce feelings of relaxation mostly for clients that may be facing stressful situations in any areas.

b) Hartland Ego-Strengthening Method, very powerful method which reinforces positive and confident suggestions and it is used in order to increase the client's confident levels.

c) Hypnotic Desensitization can be used for clients with certain phobias or anxieties which the client works with the ABC model script by writing down the present problem and the therapy goals, and during the hypnosis the client gets to a deep hypnotic relaxation suggestions to remove all the tensions followed by an imaginary scene in which the client is exposed in a deep relaxed state a couple of times and as the scene is repeated the tendency would be that he would reduce his feelings of anxiety. By inducing the client to a deep relaxed state the client will find more difficult to believe his irrational thoughts.

Repetition plays a significant role in diminishing the negative feelings, and if the client does get bored with it, it is a good sign as it means that his anxiety levels have dropped significantly.

Behavioural tasks in between sessions

The name Cognitive Behavioural Hypnotherapy clearly states the type of therapy that I will be using and its components. In order to ensure positive outcome from the therapy it is crucial that the therapist focuses on the cognitive aspect of the therapy, by identifying unhelpful beliefs or perceptions that are directly contributing for the client's distress but to also incorporate the behavioural aspect which involves practicing exposure to the stimulus in a gradual manner in order to promote behavioural changes.

It is important that during the initial consultation the therapist explains the importance of the behavioural tasks that will be assigned to him in between sessions and also to get the client's commitment to doing the homework assignment as therapy alone had proven to not be as effective as combining it with practical skills. The therapist shall be perceived as a guide to the client and the client needs to understand that the more they practice a new skill the faster they will get better.

Homework assignments should be relevant to what was learnt during the therapy, should be simple but not too easy as a degree of challenge in a gradual manner is important to achieve behavioural change. Once the client is exposed gradually to the feared stimuli, applies the learnt skills and when he can see his levels of anxiety dropping this increases the client's confidence levels not only regarding the therapy but also towards his abilities to overcome the distress he experienced.

Behavioural homework assignments can be assigned by the use of imagination or "in vivo" which is in real life. If a client suffers from social anxiety, the behavioural tasks would be related to gradually make social plans such as engaging with people or going out for dinner with a close friend.

Another example of a behavioural task assigned to a client could be a client who experiences anxiety to drive. We could agree that he would ask someone that they trust, feel comfortable and safe with to go for a short drive on a Sunday at a calm time such as early in the morning. As the client gets exposed to it we would slowly increase the distances and move to busier times gradually until the anxiety levels have dropped and he can drive alone at peak times. Note that as the client is repeatedly exposed to a stimuli the task becomes easier and easier and the anxiety levels drop until the client finally ceases to experience anxiety.

Assigning cognitive ("thinking") tasks to clients

The theory behind Cognitive Behavioural therapy is that it is not the event that causes us suffering but rather how we interpret the event that leads to distress therefore we disturb ourselves. CBT is a direct talking therapy which places a lot of importance on our perception of things, it helps the client to change how he thinks and consequently his undesired behaviour.

CBT does not place too much emphasis on the cause of the problem, it is rather interested in understanding what is maintaining the behaviour and therefore it focuses on the belief, or perception the client holds which directly influences their behaviour. In other words we perceive "why" as an unprofitable question and choose to focus on "what happens" instead.

In addition to that the role is to help the client identify the intrusive thoughts and replace them with helpful set of beliefs.

Another important aspect of CBT is that it is not the intrusive thoughts that cause distress for the client but rather the meaning the client attaches to it.

Let's assume that I am on a high building and I imagine myself jumping out of the window. In this scenario it is not the thoughts that would cause anxiety but rather how I interpret the thoughts. If I start attaching meaning to the thoughts and emphasis by interpreting them as abnormal and worrisome it will certainly affect me negatively.

However, if I identify the thoughts as SPAM and simply ignore the thoughts it will not cause any negative feelings.

It is important to train the client to develop awareness and simply identify intrusive thoughts but instead of trying to fight the thoughts, teach the client to simply let go of the thoughts.

Based on the premise that our cognition plays a major role on how we feel, it is crucial that I assign cognitive tasks to the client in between sessions in order to reinforce the ideas and for the client to get a clearer picture on his own that he is disturbing himself but to also realize that he has equal capacity to undisturb himself too.

A client who is suffering from unhealthy jealously towards his partner, the homework task I would assign would be a self-reflection regarding a recent and relevant event and use the ABCDE model in which he would analyse his negative thoughts, feelings and behaviour and replace these thoughts with helpful and logical set of new beliefs and notice how it directly influenced how he feels and therefore the behaviour too.

On the other hand, if a client is concerned about his procrastination in a certain area of his life I would recommend a Brief Problem-Solving worksheet in which he would work through the problem, goals, proposed solutions, weigh up the pros and cons of the proposed solution which would help him see the benefits of it, truly incorporate the suggested solutions and make a detailed plan and schedule to ensure that the solutions would be put into practice.

Lastly, there are clients who go to therapy however, they do not have a clearly defined goal which is an important factor as it will help both the therapist and the client to know what direction to go to, and ensure that the therapy meets the clients' expectations. In this situation I would assign the Setting SMART goals exercise as it would allow the client to have a clear understanding of what he truly wants to achieve, and the therapist to be able to guide the client to the desired direction.

Similarities and differences between Cognitive-Behavioural Hypnotherapy, Ericksonian, and Hypno-Analytic approaches to hypnotherapy.

The Erickson approach is known for the use of indirect forms of suggestion and CBH on the other hand focuses on the use of direct suggestions. Erickson's definition of hypnosis was vague and clients were often disappointed after a session as it would not go in line with their expectations. This aspect differs from CBH which provides the skills training to the client beforehand, gives a clear explanation with regards to the process and makes sure to address client's expectations, as positive expectation is crucial for successful hypnotherapy.

The Ericksonian approach is a state approach, the client is in a passive situation whereas CBH is a nonstate approach, and the client is an active participant. Both the techniques use image rehearsal and they both share the same process of induction, deepener and emerging. The CBT approach is collaborative, the client is explained the entire process and the direct suggestion makes the process explicit. In addition to that, it allows the client to give voluntary consent when responding to the suggestions. The Ericksonian technique had been criticized by deceiving the subject into believing that when under hypnosis they get into some form of trance where mysterious or magic like things may happen. This differs greatly from CBH as there is no scientific evidence that hypnosis is a "special state" and therefore the subject is in full control of it, fully aware and gives him the freedom to respond or not respond to the suggestions.

The hypno-analytical approach to hypnotherapy is a form of hypnotherapy which focuses on finding the root cause of the problem by the use of regression. Freud made use of this approach with his patients for almost a decade and had concluded that it was not effective and it may have the potential to cause harm. One of the main reasons at to why this method may not be ideal is that it can cause "retraumatization" (mostly with clients with PTSD who may re-experience the events and therefore develop anxiety) or "false memory syndrome"(as memories fade and it is not possible to measure the accuracy of the memory). This method is not consistent with the evidence-based approach due to its lack of evidence; Freud concluded that many uncovered memories from their patients were confabulated. The Hypno-analysis form of therapy tends to be a long-term form of treatment as opposed to the cognitive-behavioral approach that tends to be short-term.

On CBH various techniques are used and a very effective one is Decatastrophising imagery which promotes strong change within the client however it is a very strong technique of which clients may find it difficult to engage or uncomfortable as it goes against what he has been doing all along by facing the worst case scenario through imagery, some clients may find it particularly distressful.

The Rational Emotive Imagery, focuses on the use of imagery to help the client deal with an anxiety provoking situation by helping them create their own coping strategies as they develop "self efficacy". In order to be aware of what the client is experiencing the therapist may monitor their thoughts by asking the client questions which the client may perceive as intrusive.

Lastly, hypnotic desensitazation is widely used for the treatment of phobias and other anxiety-related disorders, the client is gradually exposed to the "threat" once he is in a deep state of relaxation. It has been observed that systematic desinsitization combined with hypnotherapy leads to a higher success rate on the treatment of the abovementioned conditions.

The difference between neurosis and psychosis and why this is relevant to hypnotherapy. Focusing on the major categories of anxiety disorder and how they may be treated differently in hypnotherapy.

One of the professional ethics with regards to therapy is that a therapist should work in his sphere of competence only, and the only way to make sure that the therapist will stick to it as by being aware of their skills and competency and also be able to distinguish the client's suitability for treatment. It is said that a successful therapist is one who can choose their client in a diligent manner. Therapists deal with clients who normally suffer from some form of psychopathology. Psychopathology can be divided into two categories: neurosis and psychosis.

In general hypnotherapists work with clients who show signs of neurosis such as social anxieties, mild addictions, and insomnia to mention a few. On the other hand clients that are suffering from psychosis need to be treated by a therapist with a multi professional approach.

A person suffering from neurosis usually exhibits a short-lived psychosis episode, he is in touch with reality and aware of the condition of which he would like to change or improve. However, a person suffering from psychosis is usually out of touch with reality, is unaware of the condition even though he is suffering from acute symptoms. In addition to that, psychosis is a condition of which affects the thinking process whereas neurosis disorders affect the emotions.

Psychosis is a clear contraindication for hypnotherapy due to the unpredictability and unstable nature of the psychotic symptoms. On the other hand it has been observed that clients suffering from psychosis are usually unresponsive to hypnotherapy. It is important to highlight that even though hypnotherapists do not diagnose nor treat psychosis they should be familiar with the subject and would also benefit from asking he client if they have been diagnosed or treated before. Some characteristics of psychosis are delusions, hallucinations, thought disorder, disorganized behaviour and negative symptoms and which makes it evident as to why hypnotherapy would not be recommended nor successful.

Neurosis is a mental illness with mild symptoms, it is not caused by organic symptoms and the person is normally in touch with reality. Even though it is the main category of disorders treated by hypnotherapists it should not be the only treatment the client shall have. Hypnotherapy is used as an auxiliary form of treatment.

The main categories of anxiety disorders are, phobias, traumatic, Obsessive-Compulsive disorders, generalized anxiety disorders and other anxiety disorders.

One of the main aspects in the treatment of neurosis is that the client shall be gradually exposed to the situation that causes him anxiety as opposed to avoiding it. Neurosis related to phobias would normally be treated with behavioural approaches mainly systematic desensitization.

An effective treatment for OCD could be Exposure Response Prevention Therapy (ERP Therapy) in which the client is gradually exposed to his fears in order to refrain from the ritual behaviour. ERT may also be effective with treating generalized anxiety disorders combined with talking CBT.

Lastly, individuals suffering from traumatic disorders may benefit from hypnotherapy through deep relaxation exercises. Hypnotherapy aids at identifying the trigger and assessing the symptoms. This helps the individual gain control and reduce the reactions to the stimuli. In addition to that it equally helps the client to identify if there are any other factors that may trigger the distress.

Fatctors that interfere with the working alliance. Nature of ruptures or problems that may occur in the therapeutic relationship and how to handle them

Therapeutic alliance plays a major role on the outcome of the therapy and therefore it is important that the therapist focuses on developing a bond with the client early in the process in which the client feels comfortable with the therapist, feels unconditional positive regard, develops trust in the therapist and therefore in the outcome of the therapy.

Working alliance is normally associated with the idea of therapeutic rapport and it refers to the relationship between the therapist and the client. Lack of rapport, trust and misunderstandings about the therapy situation may influence directly the communication during therapy as the client may become less responsive to hypnotic suggestion, less honest with the therapist and less comfortable with the therapy. In addition to that lack of congruence, being judgemental and lack of empathy may also interfere with the working alliance.

Other factors that directly impact the working alliance between the therapist and client is when the client feels like the therapist is not listening to them nor understanding them. This may lead the client to build up resistance to the therapy.

If the client feels that the therapist is not trustworthy and may break confidentiality it directly impacts their relationship as the client will not be fully opened throughout the process. Furthermore, inflexibility with regards to the treatment plan that a therapist chooses may equally have a negative impact in the working alliance. An example of this is, I personally enjoyed the "thought stopping" technique, and during a session I tried with my client who is more delicate and therefore did not enjoy the technique. He found it rather harsh and expressed preference on a more positive approach.

My role as a therapist is to check with the client and if he is not comfortable with the technique, I should be flexible enough in order to accommodate client suitability for the different forms of treatments.

In order to overcome working alliance obstacles, the therapist is advised to place great emphasis on the communication with the client. The therapist may focus on getting mutual understanding between the clients by paraphrasing and summarizing what the client is expressing. He may encourage the client to provide feedback at the end of each session, to allow the therapist to be aware of the aspects he needs to change, the therapist may show congruence, warmth and sympathy towards the client.

Communication is the key for the therapy to be effective and whenever a therapist faces obstacles he should discuss with the client and encourage the client to express themselves freely, pay attention and be flexible to make improvements.

The between state and nonstate theories of hypnosis

Prior to 1950, the hypnotherapy field was mostly dominated by state theories in which hypnosis was closely related to "hypnotic trance". Hypnosis was viewed as "special state" which the client responded to suggestions through the unconscious mind. From 1950 there was a rise on nonstate approaches which led to significant changes in practice including the development of hypnotic skills training programmes. The state approach has been a subject of criticism for nonstate theorists and modern researches mostly agree with most of the criticisms.

The state theory, derived by Mesmer's supernatural theory and the nonstate approaches derived by Braid's natural common sense theory differ in a variety of ways.

State approaches are normally the ones related to stage hypnosis, New Age Therapy whereas the nonstate it is closely linked to Cognitive-behavioural hypnotherapy and therefore it is evidence based.

In the state approach the hypnotist normally does all the work, the subject responds to suggestions with an altered state of consciousness which leads to a natural trance phenomena. The state approach hypnosis can be dangerous, it uses unique concepts, terminologies and it is more related to psychodynamic theories.

On the other hand, in the nonstate approach the client is the one that does all the work and the hypnotist simply guides the client through suggestions and therefore it is no more dangerous than ordinary suggestion.

Nonsate approaches uses psychological concepts and terminology, and suggestibility increases through positive expectations, attitude and motivation; the subject acts based on the social constructive role. The main approaches in psychology used by the hypnotists are social, cognitive and behavioural approaches.

Based on the above description we can understand why that nonstate approaches have been the preferred method since 1950. It is also clear why the nonestate approaches criticize the state approaches as the main reason that we would use hypnosis would be to achieve a result and mostly to treat neurosis.

The nonstate approach to hypnosis in which the client is aware, he learns the skills, he understands the process, he consciously responds to the suggestions would be the ideal method to work with the clients and achieve positive results. The other advantage is that in between sessions the client can use the learned skills in order to do self-hypnosis.

On a different note, takinging into account that through the state approach the client is unaware of what is done to them during hypnosis and therefore forgets what happened, this approach is not beneficial for treatment purposes as there is no skill learnt nor understanding of the process.

Moreover, in nonstate approaches the clients are taught how to respond to suggestions and they are consciously aware that their aim is to become a good hypnotic subject.

This approach is normally combined with other forms of therapy mainly CBT. There is neurological evidence that supports the nonstate approach as the "task-specific" part of the brain is observable through brain scans.

Most people view hypnosis as a state theory due to their exposure of stage hypnosis on TV and therefore are sceptical about the process. It will be beneficial for me to explain my clients the difference between the two approaches so they can get a thoroughly understanding about the subject and the nonstate approach which I will be using.

The role of evidence-based practice in hypnotherapy

Bernheiem defines hypnosis as a state of mind in which suggestion can be enhanced, in other words he argues that there is no hypnosis only suggestibility. Therefore, there is no specific feeling to hypnosis as it fully depends on the suggestions that are being given to the subject, as an example, a person who is experiencing childhood regression will certainly be experiencing hypnosis differently to a person who is engaging in a systematic desensitization hypnosis. It is however important to highlight that the history of hypnosis as well as science is not set in stone, it changes over the time as researchers find new evidence in different areas, therefore it is safer to say that there is still no evidence that hypnosis is a "special state" but it could be that we haven't found the evidence yet.

Over the years, specifically from 1950's the nature of hypnosis had changed as the scientists became more interested in the evidence based approach to hypnotherapy and the amount of research on the subject had increased. There are thousands of research papers conducted on hypnosis which solidifies the effectiveness of the nonstate approach to hypnotherapy. These research papers are based on clinical trials which have proven that the hypnotherapy techniques used can benefit the subjects and are efficient in the treatment of many conditions mainly insomnia, pain conditions and anxiety; research has also shown that if combined with CBT the treatment becomes more effective. The evidence based approach to hypnotherapy plays a significant role in the field as it makes it more likely that general practitioners will refer their patients to hypnotherapy due to the vast evidence that prove that the techniques used actually work in order to treat the presenting issues.

As a therapist, my role will be to educate my clients about the nature of hypnosis, expectations, the experience which is mainly focused attention while responding to suggestions, ensure that they are in full control of the process which means that they may choose to respond or not respond to the suggestions, the misconception about "amnesia" during the hypnotic state, the vast evidence of the efficiency of the treatment based on research and scientific studies and ensure that hypnosis is not dangerous. In addition to that I shall make him understand that there is no evidence that hypnosis is a reliable means of recovering repressed memories and therefore there is the danger that it may create false memories. It will be important to highlight the published journals which includes the British Medical Journal (BMJ) which published a "Clinical Review" where it presents an overview of the best medical research that confirms the effectiveness of hypnosis in alleviating pain and in treating vast medical conditions. Other conditions that have shown the effectiveness of hypnosis are anxiety, stress, panic disorders and insomnia which combined with CBT leads to a better outcome, phobias, obesity, acute and chronic pain and some trials have also shown its value in conditions such as asthma and in irritable bowel syndrome.

Some of the most notorious figures that have contributed to the research findings and development of the hypnotherapy field are Kirsch, Lynn, Barber, Hilgard, Nash, Banyai to mention a few. I would encourage my clients to read upon the various research findings but they must also be able to discriminate information by making sure that they are reading scientific research papers. That way they will develop trust on the methods I will be using, it will increase their positive attitude with regards to expectations and may become more motivated to use the techniques.

The typical "rules of suggestion" and other factors contributing to effective use of suggestion

Research on suggestibility and clients responses have shown that the content of which the therapist uses is not the most important factor on determining the outcome. It has been observed that the therapist plays a significant role in increasing suggestibility and therefore it is important that he appears reassuring, encouraging and confident.

The rule of suggestion are:

a) congruence, which assumes the principal that it is not what the therapist says but how he says it. As an example, if the therapist is using suggestions in a dull manner and lacking emption to the words the subject may not respond positively to the suggestions. The tone of voice is extremely powerful in comparison to what has been said, and therefore the therapist shall be in tune with what he is trying to achieve and suggest.

b) Suggestions should be positive, in other words they must be used in positive language by removing all the 'negative predicates' from a sentence. For example, instead of saying "I am not feeling stressed today" the subject can say "I am feeling calm today".

c) Present Tense, suggestions must always be phrased in the present tense such, "in the here and now" for example, "You are now becoming more and more relaxed" as the "now" is less likely to lead to ideas of possible failures as opposed to speaking on the future sense.

d) Repetition, is an important factor in learning and therefore repeating suggestions in the same manner or in different words for the same purpose my lead to achieving the same concept but from a different points of view. Hypnotists are likely to get bored with repetition but they must be aware that it is not boring for the subject and it is indeed important for them.

e) Realistic, suggestions should be realist and within the clients' sphere of control. For example saying to a school teacher, "you are now becoming a fantastic business manager" the suggestion is not realistic nor is under control of the subject.

g) Meaningfulness, clients must have an understanding on what suggestions are in order to respond, it should be used in a language the client can understand and also he needs to understand why some suggestions are made such us goal oriented suggestions in which the client imagines achieving his goal.

The different forms of hypnosis are:

a) Direct hypnosis where the therapist gives a command to the subject and the response is explicit "Your eyes are growing tired and tired and you are about to sleep",

b) indirect suggestions in which the beliefs of the subject are manipulated such as the placebo effect – an example, a client is given a sugar pill and is told that it is a pain killer which in turn cures the clients condition.

The direct form of suggestion is authoritarian as the hypnotist tells the client what to do whereas a permissive suggestion is more indirect – for example, instead of telling to client to breath slowly, the therapist can tell him to notice his breathing and keep focusing on it.

Suggestions can also take cognitive forms by the use of imagery, cognitions or it can be behavioural in which the hypnotist tells the client to do something with his body such as, elevate the arm and as it gets heavier and heavier the arm starts to drop.

The rationale, function, and application of the traditional hypnotic eye-fixation induction

The eye fixation technique is the most used induction technique in research and clinical practices. This technique was developed by James Braid in the early days and it has proven to work well with most subjects.

This technique can be briefly described as suggesting that a subject stares at an induction spot slightly higher than their normal line of vision, the subject can imagine it or stare on the ceiling with the eyes rolled back until they grow tired and naturally close. The hypnotist not only gives the instruction but he uses verbal suggestion such as "Look at me and think nothing but sleep. Your eyelids begin to feel heavy, your eyes are tired. They begin to blink, they are becoming moist, you cannot see distinctly. Your eyes closed." The hypnotist can also use commands such as "Sleep".

The Eye-Fixation induction can also be used differently in a Rapid, Modern manner of which Braid termed "a double internal upward squint", for this technique the hypnotist hold a pen above twelve inches from the subjects face and as the subject stares at it, he elevates his gaze while hypnotist uses verbal suggestions of the eyes growing tired and starting to close, followed by the command to sleep.

The rationale behind the eye-fixation technique is:

a) Focused attention, by focusing on a fixed point allows the client to avoid distractions and narrow the attention. As Braids pointed out that visual fixation leads to focused attention. This method can also contribute to help the subject to focus inward which in turn it increases suggestibility.

b) Ideo-Motor, suggestibility normally increases when it involves a muscular response too, and as the eyelids start to feel more and more tired the subject feels the eyelid muscles starting to respond and slowly closing.

c) Muscular Suggestion, as the eyelids get more tired and close, the subject may associate the response with sleepiness. This aspect could be enhanced if the subjects are trained to associate the physical sensations to its feelings. For example, eye-lids closed with sleepiness or relaxation; a smile with happiness.

d) Skills training, due to the fact that this technique is observable it allows the hypnotist to observe whether the client is complying with the suggestions, whether the eyelids do grow tired or whether the client is not responding, which can be observable if the client repeatedly looks away and gets distracted during the process.

Lastly, the eye-induction technique allows the client to learn during the therapy session and use it on their own as part of the self-hypnosis skills training. During self-hypnosis this technique can work equally well and therefore not only empowers the client but it provides them with autonomy to use and change their conditions in future situations.

The historical relationship between hypnotism and mesmerism and how it relates to modern hypnotherapy

In the eighteenth century there was a rise of a movement called Mesmerism. This movement was developed by a German doctor called Franz Mesmer who believed that there was an invisible natural energy present in all living beings. He used to charge large sums in order to provide training in the technique and therefore it passed down to very few aristocratic disciples.

It is believed that James Pool is the most notorious living person who knows about the secrets of Mesmerism. As opposed to hypnosis in which the hypnotist uses verbal suggestions and the subject responds, mesmerism uses non-verbal actions such as gaze or fascination, with the ultimate goal of inducing trance to the subject and affect the body's energy field.

This technique was referred to as "Animal Magnetism" and nowadays it can be related to things like chakra balancing, reiki, kinisieology and energy healing as these also work with invisible energy with the aim of bringing balance and manipulate it in different ways to achieve different effects.

This technique is performed to a client by putting the hands over certain parts of the body without physically touching the body or through thoughts.

During the time mesmerism suffered a lot of criticisms and it is said that their followers were often ridiculed. His techniques were not perceived as hypnosis and studies were conducted in order to test the validity of the methods.

Benjamin Frankl conducted a study in the subject and he concluded that the subjects only responded when they were aware of being magnetised. He also concluded that the animal magnetism was not a result of an energy carried by the subject but the response was due to "expectation", "belief" and "imagination", which are factors in common with effective hypnosis.

It is important to note that even though there was a vast amount of critics of the methods at the time, there was no evolution on the field for almost a century until Braid successfully developed a new perspective in the field which is evidence-based and empirical.

Braids model had soon become recognized by the British Medical Association and formally accepted by medical orthodoxy. Braid had indeed revolutionized the field of hypnotherapy with his evidence-based approach and had significant impact on the field. General Practitioners are now more inclined to refer their clients to hypnotherapy due to the vast amount of scientific evidence that proves its effectiveness.

It is important to highlight that Mesmerism and Hypnotism are not the same concept and differ greatly in a number of ways and one of the main differences is that in Mesmerism the operator induces the subject without suggestions, it is perceived as supernatural, it leads to trance, can be performed in secret or at a distance and subjects acquire supernatural powers.

On the other hand hypnotism is rational, scientific, it induces nervous fatigue, it requires full knowledge and participation of the subject and subjects simply enhance normal abilities.

The relationship between comedy stage hypnosis and modern hypnotherapy. Strategies and techniques used in stage hypnosis to mislead the audience

Most people tend to assume that individuals during stage hypnosis are under a "special state" that makes them behave in a certain manner, and therefore most people form their conception about hypnosis based on stage demonstrations usually exposed on TV shows for entertainment purposes.

It has been observed that the apparent success in hypnosis during stage demonstrations is usually more apparent than real. This form of hypnosis is usually responsible for people's misconceptions about the nature of hypnosis. It is very often that people tell me that they are scared of being hypnotised as they fear revealing unwanted information or do things that they wouldn't feel comfortable doing in their normal state.

This gives me the opportunity to explain that the hypnotherapy that I will be performing is evidence-based, it is conducted for therapy and treatment purposes as opposed to stage hypnosis which is done purely for entertainment purposes.

One of the most known figures of stage hypnosis is Darren Brown, he does an incredible work in convincing the audience about his success in hypnosis however, his techniques have not been tested with regards to its accuracy.

When it comes to Hypnotherapy the only act available is "The Hypnotism Act 1952" related to stage hypnosis, referred as "public entertainment". This act states that hypnosis can only be performed with a license which is authorized by the local authority.

The act prohibits hypnosis to be conducted to any person under the age 18, the hypnotist should also ensure suitability for participation and therefore the hypnotist shall first address this to the audience before starting the performance. In addition to that, the act also includes "prohibited actions" and hypnotic or post-hypnotic suggestions should be completely removed from the mind of the subject and audience before the end of the show.

This act plays a significant role in protecting the participants based on the premise that there was no initial consultation which is important in order to ensure no harm.

McGill published "New Encyclopaedia of Stage Hypnosis" where he details a vast amount of the traditional tricks mostly used by stage hypnosis. Some of the variables used by stage hypnotists are selection of extraverted and hyper-suggestible subjects, they are able to select the subjects by using some tests that measure suggestibility and that allows them to quickly spot the most suitable subjects to go on stage, they benefit from being charismatic and authoritarian as it will attract the audience more. They also make use of deception, by deliberately using "sleight of hand" which is based on magic tricks and illusions to mislead the audience.

Some of the techniques used for deception include, Private whispers, by whispering to the subject off the microphone to ask for their compliance to deceive the audience by suggestions such as "play along"; they deliberately don't challenge the audience as an example, instead of saying "try to bend your finger" they will say "your finger is so stiff that you cannot bend it"; they use fake hypnosis tricks used by trickers, fakirs, illusionists and mentalists.

The evidence-based approach is similar with this approach in the fact that they also select the clients based on suitability, the use of suggestions and confidence in the approach.

Hypnotists also need to believe in their approach considering that it is evidence-based and the percentage of successful treatments is very high.

On a different note, the evidence-based approach makes the use of induction whereas stage hypnotists either don't use it or use "instant induction".

References

Brookes.ac.uk. (2017). *Reflective writing: About Gibbs reflective cycle - Oxford Brookes University*. [online] Available at: https://www.brookes.ac.uk/students/upgrade/study-skills/reflective-writing-gibbs/ [Accessed 15 Jun. 2017].

Brookhouse, S. (2017). *Neurosis and Psychosis is There a Difference - Hypnotherapy Manchester*. [online] Brookhouse Hypnotherapy Manchester. Available at: https://hypnomanchester.co.uk/neurosis-and-psychosis-is-there-a-difference/ [Accessed 24 Jun. 2017].

College, C. (2017). *Clinical supervision - UK College of Clinical Hypnosis*. [online] UK College of Clinical Hypnosis. Available at: http://www.ukcch.org.uk/clinical-supervision/ [Accessed 16 Jun. 2017].

Eason, A. (2017). *Hypnotic Susceptibility Scales and the Notion Of Suggestibility*. [online] Adam Eason. Available at: http://www.adam-eason.com/hypnotic-susceptibility-scales-and-the-notion-of-hypnotisability-or-suggestibility/ [Accessed 13 Jun. 2017].

Eason, A. (2017). *Reflective Practice In Hypnotherapy*. [online] Adam Eason. Available at: http://www.adam-eason.com/reflective-practice-in-hypnotherapy-something-all-hypnotherapists-should-be-doing/ [Accessed 15 Jun. 2017].

General-hypnotherapy-register.com. (2017). *Supervision & CPD Policy | General Hypnotherapy Standards Council & General Hypnotherapy Register*. [online] Available at: http://www.general-hypnotherapy-register.com/supervision-cpd-policy/ [Accessed 16 Jun. 2017].

Giovannilordi.com. (2017). *What is Mesmerism? How is it Used? My Experiences Using it With Hypnosis.*. [online] Available at: http://www.giovannilordi.com/blog/mesmerism-what-is-it-how-is-it-used-my-experiences [Accessed 27 Jun. 2017].

Lifelong Learning with OT. (2017). *Guide to models of reflection – when & why should you use different ones?*. [online] Available at:
https://lifelonglearningwithot.wordpress.com/2016/05/02/different-models-of-reflection-using-them-to-help-me-reflect/ [Accessed 15 Jun. 2017].

Mark Tyrrell's Therapy Skills. (2017). *3 Ways to Communicate Client Responsibility in Therapy*. [online] Available at: http://www.unk.com/blog/3-ways-to-communicate-client-responsibility/ [Accessed 13 Jun. 2017].

Mesmerism.com. (2017). *Mesmerism | The original and most successful form of hypnosis*. [online] Available at: http://www.mesmerism.com/ [Accessed 27 Jun. 2017].

Nyccognitivebehavioraltherapy.com. (2017). *CBT Homework Assignments | Cognitive Behavioral Therapist*. [online] Available at: http://nyccognitivebehavioraltherapy.com/cbt-homework-assignments/ [Accessed 24 Jun. 2017].

Ocdaction.org.uk. (2017). *What Is Cognitive Behavioural Therapy (CBT)? | OCD Action | The UK's Obsessive Compulsive Disorder Charity*. [online] Available at: http://www.ocdaction.org.uk/resource/what-cognitive-behavioural-therapy-cbt [Accessed 24 Jun. 2017].

Primaltherapy.com. (2017). *Grand Delusions - Chapter 2*. [online] Available at:

http://www.primaltherapy.com/GrandDelusions/GD02.htm [Accessed 24 Jun. 2017].

Robertson, D. (2013). *The Practice of Cognitive-behavioural Hypnotherapy: A Manual for Evidence-based Clinical Hypnosis.* Karnac Books.

Selfgrowth.com. (2017). *The rationale, function, and application of the traditional hypnotic eye-fixation induction.* [online] Available at: http://www.selfgrowth.com/articles/the-rationale-function-and-application-of-the-traditional-hypnotic-eye-fixation-induction [Accessed 27 Jun. 2017].

Zimberoff, D. (2017). *How to Treat PTSD With Hypnotherapy.* [online] Web.wellness-institute.org. Available at: http://web.wellness-institute.org/blog/bid/258833/treating-ptsd-with-hypnotherapy [Accessed 24 Jun. 2017].

Zimberoff, D. (2017). *How to Treat PTSD With Hypnotherapy.* [online] Web.wellness-institute.org. Available at: http://web.wellness-institute.org/blog/bid/258833/treating-ptsd-with-hypnotherapy [Accessed 24 Jun. 2017].

CHAPTER 3

Overcoming Procrastination

If we use the average life expectancy in 1st world countries such as the UK the average life expectancy is 79.5, equivalent to 29037 days.

On average people spend one third of their lives asleep which is equivalent to 318 months.

This gives you 636 months left to live.

On average a person spends 15 years in education which is equivalent to 43 months (excluding weekends).

From 19 to 65 working, this totals 128 months of your life spend working.

20 minutes in the toilet a day which sums up to 13 months and 1 week.

On averaged 5 meals per day, which gives an estimate of 6 years of your life eating.

The average person spends 5 years waiting in lines and queues where roughly 6 months of that is waiting at traffic lights.

On average 4 years doing housework, 1 year looking for lost possessions and two weeks of our lifetime kissing another person.

Now let's contemplate on the following: How have you been spending the 12 years that you may have left but not guaranteed? Do you spend doing nothing?

While we don't have much control of these factors we do have control of other areas of our lives and the question is, do we use our time wisely? The obvious answer to this is that some of us don't. Most of us procrastinate.

V.　How much time in our lives to spend procrastinating?

Let's look at what procrastination actually means.

"A behaviour that you put off to do it later at a time that it is in your interest to do it at a particular time. So it's not a matter of planned delay but a delay that it is not in the person's interest." Windy Dryden

Procrastination can be especially problematic when putting off important tasks, such as paying the bills, or applying for jobs. There are a number of causes of excessive procrastination.

Some people do not place enough focus on planning; they did not develop the habit of planning to complete a task which usually involves breaking it into chunks and therefore may easily get very overwhelmed with large projects. Feeling overwhelmed usually leads to avoidance, and the longer we avoid the tasks, the higher the probability of developing anxiety, increases the negative feelings resulting in more procrastination.

There are other factors that play a role in procrastination namely anxiety, self-esteem, attention problems, as well as other skills deficits.

The interesting part is the rationalizations that people make:

1. I don't have enough material to start this task
2. I am not in the right mood to start this task
3. I need motivation to start this task
4. I am not going to do it until I am ready to do it
5.

Procrastination has three major features:

1. The task is in our interest to do;
2. A timeframe which is important for us to take action;
3. A postponement of this action until another time;

So what do people normally do?

4. Either at the very last minute;
5. After the due deadline;
6. Action is not taken at all;

The areas we procrastinate the most:

- Personal maintenance (health, personal cleanliness, finance, work);
- Self-development (developing personal interests, improving opportunities in our chosen line of work, gaining further educational qualifications and broadening knowledge in specific and/general areas);
- Honoring commitments to others;

As I mentioned above, every one of us have procrastinated at some point in our lives and it is extremely common. However, sometimes things get really bad if we are dealing with Chronic Procrastination.

There are two types of chronic procrastination, namely:

- Chronic specific procrastination (we tend to have a long-standing problem doing things on time in one area of our lives but in other areas the problem is not predominant);
- Chronic general procrastination (we tend to procrastinate in a number of important areas in our lives, it has been going on for years that has become part of our daily lives – this is a more difficult form to overcome).

The good news:

You can help yourself overcome both types of procrastination.

Bad news:

You will not find it easy to do so.

Procrastination itself is a habit, a bad habit indeed, and habits take time to break. There is no getting around it. If you are willing to break the habit, all you need to have is the following:

- Awareness – you are in fact procrastinating.
- Goal-directness – a wish to have the task done.
- Persistence – willingness to repeat the procedures until it becomes second nature for you.

The good news is:

You do already have the skills present in you, you have it. I won't have to teach you the skills, I am only going to teach you how to use them in ways that will be of utmost benefit for you. I shall motivate you to shift the skills to the areas that are more important to you which will allow you to live a more meaningful life that is not characterized by avoidance and self-deception.

Three Themes:

1. The theme of avoiding discomfort (most predominant and normally present together with the other themes and therefore avoidance.)
2. Avoiding tasks that remind you of your own inadequacies, as a result you put off the time until you feel more confident to do the task. There is an

ego-threat with the behaviour of doing something that it is in your interest to do.

3. "I will do it when I choose to do it", and not when anybody else chooses me to do it. "I will show you that I am autonomous and I will do it when I choose to do it"; "I MUST be free";

People usually asks me when is the best time to complete a task and take action and I normally answer as follows:

"The best time to take action is right now."

If we continue to wait until the right time to do things we will never get there… we will continue looking for excuses to postpone things as its basically impossible to find a perfect time where all the conditions are perfect to take action.

The bad news is that we have no control over the external circumstances, the good news is that we have control over our perception of the events which directly influences how we feel and how we respond to things.

As one of my Favourite Psychologists stated:

"Everything can be taken from a man but one thing: the last of the human freedoms—to choose one's attitude in any given set of circumstances, to choose one's own way."

Viktor Frankl

Now let's briefly look at ways that can help you to overcome procrastination.

VI.   Overcoming Procrastination:

1. Specific goals (Be as specific as possible – when, where, for how long, at what time, how many days a week...)
2. Using the 5 minute CBT technique for procrastination rule –apply everyday... if you stop after the 5 minutes every day we can revise it and change it to 10 minutes.
3. Define rewards and penalties (i.e. financial – money to charity; Hygiene – not take a shower for the day...)
4. Create a Prioritized To Do list "Urgent", "Moderately important", "Put off until later" (can help you make an informed choice on what things to put off and when, rather than finishing the easier things first).
5. Use your natural patterns to your advantage, if you are more alert in the mornings, schedule more difficult tasks in the mornings. Do you feel more desire to interact with people after lunch? Schedule lunch meetings or phone calls then. Is there a time of day you prefer to be in silence and spend some alone time? That may be a good time for organizing your things. Chances are if you don't like doing a particular task at a certain time, you are more likely to put it off.

6.   What would stop you from achieving this goal?

Coaching is normally used with people who are well established in life but are inclined to achieve excellence in certain areas of their lives. Coaching usually helps by setting some goals and help you getting a plan to deal with it.

In a case study Peter had just got a new job and he has asked for coaching in order to ensure that he increases his performance and together we did the goal-setting and the plan of action.

And in between the time, he heard that his twin brother had been diagnosed with cancer and he is now preoccupied; now we find that there is an obstacle, and he comes back asking for advice as we planned to work in a specific area however that is what happened which will interfere with our coaching objective. Me as a coach I acknowledge that it is an obstacle to our work and I use the REBT framework which explains that it has nothing to do with the coaching objective. Why? Because life is like that, life doesn't say: This person is in coaching, let's keep the adversities away from him because he deserves to be focused on the coaching in order to get great value in it. Unless you have connections with God to clear your way... life has a funny tendency to give you adversities when you least expected.

So what is the process of dealing with the obstacles?

- You identify and agree with the coachee that it is an obstacle and that it is interfering with the coaching objective. And that it needs to be addressed before that pursuit can be resumed.
- You come to an agreement with the coachee of what is the nature of these obstacles.

There are two types of obstacles:

1. Practical obstacles;
2. Emotional obstacle;

If you have a practical obstacle you may have emotional obstacles related to the practical obstacle

Tips:

Complete the tasks immediately, as opposed to leaving small "To Do" tasks for later i.e. Promise the client to email something – email instantly.

Increase Pressure (Put a timer for faster tasks that you normally take longer to complete... it may bring anxiety but it will help overcoming the long periods that takes to complete a task)

VII.   School environment

Student life usually entails lots of work to be done with constant deadlines and failure to honour the commitments usually have automatic negative consequences such as getting lower marks and in the worst case scenario failing the grade.

One of the main reasons that leads to underperformance within the student's environment are procrastination which is directly related to the lack of goal setting, demotivation, and also lack of participation in classes due to anxiety for public speaking.

Public speaking is one of the most common type of neurosis and it may easily influence underperformance as the student may need further understanding which may only be achieved by asking questions during the classes as well as participating. Anxiety related conditions and how to overcome them will be explained in detail during the sessions.

When it comes to procrastination, this is something that most students do it unconsciously as they find ways to rationalize the reasons as to why it is not the right time to get things done. They can easily come up with the idea that they need to clean the house, they think they still have time to do it and therefore they can leave it for later, they may all of a sudden believe that they are too tired to focus and therefore they will wake up earlier to study for an exam for example, they may decide to fall in love and may appear unable to focus on work to mention a few.

My aim is to help you uncover your potential, beat procrastination and allow yourself to achieve excellence.

On the other hand – this is a crucial time to focus on making the right decisions as the decisions that will be made today will determine what the rest of our lives will look like.

Guidance and being sure to choose the right career path, based on you gifts, passion, tendencies, skills and abilities is by far one of the most important decisions in our lives.

Let's assume again that the average time that we will live is 80 years old, note that if you start working at the age of 22 hypothetically you will basically work until you are about 60 year old, this leaves the timeframe of 48 years spent in working in a job that goes hand in hand on either you hate it or love it.

As the philosopher Alan Watts stated: *The essential principle of business, of occupation in the world is figure out some way in which you get paid for playing.*

"This is the real secret of life -- to be completely engaged with what you are doing in the here and now and instead of calling it work, realize it is play"

As a teenager, during my university years, every single time that it was exams time – I used to sit with my best-friend and look at the career book to try and change it as I was unsure of what I wanted. I failed many times, but over the years I grew a passion for the field but have only taken the step to follow the dream after 10 years. Again, if I had any kind of guidance I would have probably taken the step a lot earlier or I could have chosen another career that would allow me to be more balanced, get better results and make better decisions.

Failing is something that can easily be avoided through studying and less procrastination.

If we are to make such decisions that will impact the rest of our lives, how about focusing, understanding fully what we really want from life, our passion and basically ask ourselves:

What would I want to do if money were no object?

Let's take a moment to understand, how do you perceive your education and the process of studying?

Do you look at it as something that you hate but needs to be done as you feel like you have no other choice?

Do you look at it as "studying" or "learning"?

When you do experience a sense of overwhelm due to the amount of tasks to be done? What do you tell yourself regarding it?

Do you have a competitive nature?

Do you find yourself comparing your results to your colleagues and does it bring any sense of inadequacy or ego-boosting from your side?

When you do have tasks to complete which are in your interest to do in a certain timeframe what do you tell yourself that leads to procrastination?

What are your favourite subjects?

Which subjects are you good at?

What do you do during your free time? Is there anything you would wish to do more but continuously find excuses to not have it done, such as going to the gym?

Where do you see yourself in the next 10 years?

Are you taking any action that will facilitate your goal on where you would like to be in future?

CHAPTER 4

Overcoming Anxiety

In 2019 the world was woke up to the news of novel, deadly and highly contagious virus that started in Wuhan (China) on the news named as Covid-19. At the time China had classified it as an epidemic and with immediate effect closed all boarders from Wuhan to other cities in China in order to ensure that it would not spread it through the country.

What their government did not do was to close its boarders to other countries worldwide which meant that within a few months we were indeed dealing with a Pandemic. The numbers started to rise at an alarming worldwide, Donald Trump had decided to close the borders in the USA to most countries which was highly criticized globally but not long after, most countries closed their boards as an effort to reduce the spreading between countries and avoid mutations of the virus as well.

Unfortunately within months new and more deadly variants started to appear in certain countries such as South Africa, India, Brazil and United Kingdom. This unexpected pandemic created great panic throughout the world, due to the sudden negative changes, curfews, the use of masks and desifectants regularly throughout the day, keeping distance from one another, limited gatherings, not being able to hug another anymore, loss of millions of jobs worldwide, the worries and uncertainties that came with it.

There is no doubts that it had affected a large majority of us on a great scale. The constant news related to the pandemic has been excessive and unfortunately it may lead to a strong impact in our mental health and even stronger for the ones who already have the tendencies to experience anxiety and OCD (Obsessive-compulsive disorder).

Now let's take a look at the Mental Health aspect of things.

Among many different conditions that I have been working with over the years, Anxiety is to a great extent the most experienced condition by a large majority of people.

Cognitive Behavioural Therapy has been perceived as the 'Golden therapy' as it is the most effective and widely-used treatment approach for anxiety related disorders.

What is anxiety in a nutshell?

Anxiety is an emotion that we tend to experience when our minds or bodies perceive a threat or danger. It is mainly connected to our belief system.

Unhealthy thoughts lead to unhealthy emotions and therefore it directly reflects in our behaviour. It is very important to understand that – because our mind/body perceives it as a threat by no means it means that it is accurate.

Rule number 1:

Do not blindly believe in everything that you think nor feel. We are not our thoughts. Thoughts are random, thoughts can be helpful, rational, irrational, unhelpful, non-sense, and our mind loves to play with thoughts. Our duty is to be fully aware of those thoughts and before believing them and responding to them – test them.

This is what I call: Being the Master of your own mind. Not a slave. Understanding and Training our minds is one of the most important tasks we shall invest time and effort into. Our Minds have the power of being our best-friend and equal power to be our worst enemy. The choice is ours.

Some of the characteristics of Anxiety are:

(1) To overestimate negative features

(2) Underestimates someone's ability to cope with the threat

(3) Creates an even more negative threat in one's mind

(4) Has more task irrelevant thoughts and therefore behaviours

(5) Constantly seeking reassurance.

As a Rational Emotive Behavioural Therapist (REBT), my aim is usually to move you from anxiety to concern.

Some of the characteristics of concern are:

(1) To view the threat realistically

(2) Realistic appraisal of our ability to cope with the threat

(3) Does not create an even more negative threat in one's mind

(4) Has more task relevant thoughts than anxiety

(5) To face up to the threat as well as deal with it constructively.

If you observe the differences between Anxiety and Concern you may conclude that experiencing concern is also a negative emotion but it is a healthy negative emotion that is more rational, helpful, logical and beneficial as opposed to anxiety.

Taking into account the very difficult times that we are currently facing as well as our loved ones it is natural that we experience negative emotions - afterall we are humans. My aim is to simply point out that we can experience it in a healthier manner that shall not lead to emotional disturbance such as panics, anxieties nor behaviours such as buying the entire store.

So what measures can we take that shall be more beneficial for our Mental Health?

- Be mindful about what you read and try to limit the news; so you can allow yourself to focus on other areas too. We do have other areas of our lives that we value too and we shall work towards finding balance in our minds;

- Be aware of your thoughts and if there are any recurrent thoughts that may be contributing to the negative emotions you shall be experiencing — explore it. You may set a specific time to dedicate to the news and be aware that there is a lot of misinformation too and therefore please place your focus on the trusted sources;

- Try to have a break from social media too as it can easily work as trigger too;

- Wash your hands, in a mindful manner but not excessively. Try to be aware with regards to what drives you to wash your hands. Is it for health safety precautions or is it becoming compulsive instead?

Try to be mindful and not exaggerate as remember that our brain's seems to have a PHD on clinging into habits as long as you repeat it enough, somehow it becomes automatic without us realizing it and we shall unnecessarily develop OCD (Obsessive-compulsive disorder) tendencies.

- Stay Connected with people, if you are going through the isolation process on your own – try to take some time to stay connected with your loved ones and check on each other.

- Take this time as an opportunity, to spend quality time with yourself and possibly some good rest. Remember all those times that you were not able to fully focus on your goals, take time for yourself, and focus on your journey because you were too busy with life? If you do suddenly have the time now, try to focus on the here and now - where you are at the moment and where you are aiming to go?

- Avoid burnout, the length and developments of the epidemic highly increases the probability of feeling low at times. Please ensure to access nature, try to get some sunlight whenever it is possible. Try to exercise, eat well and stay hydrated.

Practice the "Apple" technique to deal with anxiety and worries.

Acknowledge: Notice and acknowledge the uncertainty as it comes to mind.

Pause: Don't react as you normally do. Don't react at all. Pause and breathe.

Pull back: Tell yourself this is just the worry talking, and this apparent need for certainty is not helpful and not necessary. It is only a thought or feeling. Don't believe everything you think. Thoughts are not statements or facts.

Let go: Let go of the thought or feeling. It will pass. You don't have to respond to them. You might imagine them floating away in a bubble or cloud.

Explore: Explore the present moment, because right now, in this moment, all is well. Notice your breathing and the sensations of your breathing. Notice the ground beneath you. Look around and notice what you see, what you hear, what you can touch, what you can smell. Right now. Then shift your focus of attention to something else - on what you need to do, on what you were doing before you noticed the worry, or do something else - mindfully with your full attention.

I wish you strength, hope, focus, humbleness, good health to you and your family and a sense of unity. I shall highlight that we shall only be able to conquer this virus if we work collectively and each of us takes the necessary steps to protect each other.

If you find yourself with low mood, anxiety, stress, depressed, among other feelings and would like to learn more about the main approaches that I use namely, Cognitive Behavioural Therapy & Hypnotherapy, Eastern Philosophy, Logotherapy, NLP and Life Coaching and would like to find out how it can benefit you, I do encourage you to reach out to me.

Many studies, including the 2014 study published in Behavioural Research and Therapy found that online CBT is effective in treating anxiety disorders.

CHAPTER 5

Covid-19: Our Greatest Teacher

As we experience the Global Health Crisis due to the spreading of the Coronavirus throughout the world, I would like to wish you Strength, Good Health and Hope for you and your family.

As I concluded my intensive retreat in "Discovering Buddhism" at Kopan Monastery in Nepal, the master told us:

"Now that you have concluded the program, if you would like to test your tolerance levels and your progress I advise you to go to India".

This is to say that, there is great value in practicing to elevate our frustration tolerance, eliminate or at least minimize our poisonous thoughts to a level that they no longer disturb is. Getting exposed to stressful circumstances can be diligently used as an opportunity to test and practice our capacity for tolerance as well as patience.

For those who have worked with me before, you shall be aware that as a Rational Emotive Behavioural Therapist, we believe that some of the main causes that lead to Emotional Disturbance are Low-Frustration tolerance and Awfulising. In other words, perceiving events as "the end of the world bad" and I have always highlighted the importance of increasing our frustration tolerance. I challenge you to use this unique opportunity to test your progress and to work on increasing it.

Let's play the game! Have you heard the saying:

If you cannot beat your enemy, join it?

"Some Buddhist practitioners would spend a considerate amount of time making mandala art with sand, focusing on every single detail. Once they finish the beautiful art, they destroy the work with their hands. This exercise is normally done to practice understanding the impermanence of everything. The demand for permanence in every area of our existence is the cause of human misery because there is no such thing as permanence at all." – On the Road to Enlightenment, Sharlene Raston.

Coronavirus has arrived to provide pure evidence of impermanence and give us the opportunity to reflect on how fragile we are and life is. And how strong the universe and nature is – it is random, it does as it pleases, it does not discriminate and I do hope that we have now understood that having "control" of things is an illusion.

When it comes to nature, the weather is the perfect example to show that it is very difficult do accurately predict. The most interesting prediction of the weather is when it says 50% chance of rain - it might rain or it might not!

 If one day our ego had made us believe that we are special, stronger, unbeatable or higher, I hope that coronavirus had allow us to see that our ego has been deceiving us.

How many species have been extinct until today?

How quick is an earthquake to cause mass destruction?

Does it look difficult for nature?

What makes us think that we are more special than all the previous civilizations and living beings that no longer exist?

The most difficult events that have happened in my life were absolutely crucial to where I am today. The interesting part about the feelings of despair that we experience when our security is taken away from us is that we begin to believe that we have nothing to lose. The energy that we used during our entire lives to maintain our illusion of "security" is no longer applicable, as we

realise that it is nothing more than an illusion
and we surrender. When we do reach this stage,
something Magical happens - we suddenly have access to
deposits of energy that shall be used into building the
new.

We no longer need catastrophes to happen in our lives to
follow the very same principal. Nature is natural, natural is
not forceful and from the moment we try to control the
process we interrupt the process.

As an example, we cannot open a rose to open faster, we
interrupt the process. We have to wait until it naturally
opens. In other words, from the moment that we let it be,
it shall flourish in due time.

As we go through difficult periods it is of high importance
to understand that the bright times do come. But what
we choose to do during the difficult times is what
determines the "success" later in life or when the bright
times do arrive.

When you water your plants and you care for them daily -
the end result is inevitably flowers or fruits - it comes
inevitably and naturally. There are even seasons for each
"fruit".

Lastly, as I reflect about Life and the Universe there is one
thing that I have observed and has made a great difference
into how I process things. There are no good or bad
events, there are only events. We do not know if
something is a misfortune or fortune because things
unfold with time and we cannot understand them as we

look forward, but we definitely will understand when we do look backwards.

Alan Watts explains this concept beautifully on the story below:

"The Story of a Chinese Farmer"

*Once upon a time there was a Chinese farmer whose horse ran away. That evening, all of his neighbors came around to commiserate. They said, "We are so sorry to hear your horse has run away. This is most unfortunate." The farmer said, "**Maybe**." The next day the horse came back bringing seven wild horses with it, and in the evening everybody came back and said, "Oh, isn't that lucky. What a great turn of events. You now have eight horses!" The farmer again said, "**Maybe**."*

*The following day his son tried to break one of the horses, and while riding it, he was thrown and broke his leg. The neighbours then said, "Oh dear, that's too bad," and the farmer responded, "**Maybe**." The next day the conscription officers came around to conscript people into the army, and they rejected his son because he had a broken leg. Again all the neighbours came around and said, "Isn't that great!" Again, he said, "**Maybe**."*

The whole process of nature is an integrated process of immense complexity, and it's really impossible to tell whether anything that happens in it is good or bad —

"Because you never know what will be the consequence of the misfortune; or, you never know what will be the consequences of good fortune." — Alan Watts

CHAPTER 6

Existence: Searching For the Truth

What I find most astonighing when conversing with people is questions such as: "Do you believe in G-d?", "What is your view on who G-d is?" or "I believe that....", "In my view its...." as if we are dealing with perspective.

The new trend is: "I am G-d" – I have fallen into that theory in the past until I really reflected on it and of course I am not G-d. I could perhaps say that my body is a temple where the Holy Spirit resides in.

Having studied philosphy the past 20 years and having encountered plenty of theories I learnt that when one develops one they are very good in persuading it and for as long as we do not deepen it and understand more - it is very easy to fall into a well developed theory and specially if it is music to the ear and perceived as "cool".

Why does the question: "Do you believe in G-d?" sounds unprofitable to me? Because it is not about believing but rather it is or it isn't. For example: "Do you believe that there is life on other planets?" Again - this is not "I believe..." but rather there is or there isn't" So the appropriate answer to that is: "I do not know if there is life on other planets..." not "I don't believe...". My perspective on things does not change the facts.

The creation of theories nowadays regarding existence is highly applauded which is great, we are being creative but the issue I find is that it is now perceived as the truth as opposed to what it actually is - a theory or an idea. And when we do this - we are in fact being dogmatic - religious to our own theories and ready to defend it. Atheists are very religious about their beliefs and make sure to express it and convert people too. Take a moment to observe.

We all worship something – and becomes a G-d to us. And by this I mean – we all serve something. Some worship and serve Money, others the pursuit of Happiness, others wellness - as I like to say the wellness pandemic, others worship their Ego, themselves - through Nacissism, others society and its ideas of beauty, others food, others vanity, others science, others serve God the Creator and his laws.

I recall being invited for speeches and when I discuss prior – my findings after working with hundreds of people and evaluating their similarities and differences, success rate and the length of it which includes having God in their lives or not - I am told to say something else as people are very resistant, block and therefore I shall replace it with "universe" for example, pray to the universe for help with "anxiety" as opposed to developing a relationship with the

Creator of the universe, our Maker. And I ask - why would one pray to the universe as opposed to the Creator of the universe? Who is best to guide us, comfort us other than our Creator? If I am asked to give a recommendation of a book to read, if I say Mark Mason, Robin Sharma... I am the best and super cool. If I say – go read the Word of God, the Scriptures – ohh I am terrible. Although the ones that do – you actively see their transformation and it is astonishing too.

Among other examples - I found that people are more concerned about hearing what they want to hear, the whole "cool universe trend" than to really get in touch with the truth.

As for the Worshipers of Science which includes the Darwin's Theory - it is even more interesting how it gets defended with claws – when science is the one field that is forever changing which includes the Public Health sector. The disagreements are HUGE. And up to today - the greatest thinkers and developers of the most efficient theories such as Psychologist Marsha M. Linehan – developer of the Dialectical Behavioural Therapy openly stated that we may have found the best methods to treat certain conditions, it is the BEST but it is still not good enough. So someone shall pull back and focus more and more on research.

My research started when I actively realised that science is not set in stone AT ALL and it has serious limitations if the idea is to actively cure. But at the same time - I can sadly understand why they do this, if people don't get messed up and get successfully cured - there shall be a great loss of customers. What will happen to one of the RICHEST if not the richest corporations worldwide IF people are healthy? What will happen to their revenue? The BIG Pharma is a business full stop.

The simple shift to one feeling worthy, perceive our nature as human beings as enough and precious, self-confidence, self-acceptance and love— how many industries would get affected?

As opposed to humans - animals are the ones that are simply content with who they are.

Nowadays how many people are sick? How many relationships and marriages have split? How many people are on medication? How many people are struggling with Mental Health WORLDWIDE?

The latest research findings show that the highest cause of disease, lower imune system, proneness to illnesses is loneliness. And what are they promoting daily to the point of forcing it upon people? Loneliness and lack of connections.

CHAPTER 7

Has Love been corrupted?

It is so astonishing that love appears to be such a problem that God had to transfom into a commandment: "Love thy neighbour" – how sad is that? But as a philosopher and psychotherapist who deals with many couples – that somehow forced me to look into things on a very deep level, understand what went wrong with people and why so many marriages are falling apart by the day. I found that the concept of Love is highly corrupted and it is indeed a very selfish emotion. And let me give you an illustration of this: We Love the other person for as long as they treat us in a certain manner that makes us feel good. So it is not about "you" it is about "me". From the very moment that you no longer make me feel a certain way determined by me - you are no longer deserving of my Love. In general the tendency may lead to blocking the object of love, feelings of anger, hate and the object may equally transform into an enemy. So I do not Love you - I Love the way you make me feel.

We have reached a point that Love had become the object of worship. And by saying this I equally include the concept of 'marrying for Love'. These two do not go hand in hand. Marriage is stability and permanent. Love is an emotion - and therefore, unstable and impermanent. How do human-beings rationalize mostly? "I Love you, you love me, let's get married" – This is the greatest recipe for a disaster by the simple fact that Love being an emotion means that it shall fluctuate between the couple; it is selfish as it is based on how you make me feel. Result: "I do not feel the same way anymore", "I do not love you the same anymore", "I am under the impression that you do not love me as you used to" – Time to separate.

You ask: "What led to your separation/divorce? I no longer feel the same way anymore" – this is absolutely expected and its obvious it would happen at some point.... So, if a marriage is decided to take place on the basis of love only – the probability of survival for a lifetime as pretended is low.

Hence my statment that the idea of Love – has been currupted and may have long-term negative effects.

Now we can get back to the commandment: "Love thy neighbour and Love your enemies" – Now we are speaking. Because this means that it is no longer a selfish love and based on how the other makes me feel. It is genuine unconditional love - in other words, not conditioned by circumstances. If we simply love those who love us and make us feel good, how do we differ from others. When God sends rain or sunshine he sends it to everyone not to the righteous only, he is graceful. When we are able to share the same qualities as our Father in Heaven we become his children and this allows us to stand out as we wear the crown of the Kingdom of God.

For as long as love will continue to be selfish – It simply means that we will contribute and focus on things that bring us an advantage and of course we won't care about the Ocean cause it makes no difference to one's life.

Rhino poaching and trophy hunting will mean zero – as it doesnt make any difference to one's life.

The idea I am promoting is: To Evaluate what we actually mean by "Love". How have we been behaving towards the emotion of "Love" and "To what extent has it been a selfish emotion in our own private lives".

Marrying for Love is no better than marrying for money. You are not marrying the person, you are marrying the Love they provide and how it makes you feel. If the tap is closed here and there – the marriage shall fall apart. This is to say: We do not marry the person just the Love.

This is what went wrong.

Now I am not suggesting in any way that Love shall not be present in a marriage – of course it should. But it must come from a different route. You are my husband/wife and therefore important to me, the degree of importance is unchangeable. Love transforms into an ideal tool to have a successful and happy marriage. Whether the Love fluctuates or not –It makes no difference as the degree of your importance in my life is unchangeable. Now we are forming a solid ground to stand on with the feeling of love.

Another point I wanted to make is that there are many approaches to relationship / marriage counselling and many of them very detailed and full of psychology in them and many of them are famous too. And as I have been working and observing couples and the choice of approach they use - I realized that regardless of how much all those theories make sense and appear very knowledgeable it did not transform their marriage or bring a significant transformation regardless of how much they read – even if there was improvement - but it would be temporary. And we equally know that the stats of these countries that follow these western perspectives, have a high divorce rate. Which led me to conclude that there is a strong solid ground that is not getting built and the approaches are not effective.

After that, I started thinking about the cultures that tend to have much lower divorce rate - and clearly they MUST be doing something different and much more effective.

According to the journal published in March 2008 by Allen S. Maller, Jewish Educators vs Mixed Marriages, "*Those people who are low on the Jewish ritual index have a divorce rate of 32 percent; the medium observers are in the middle with a 16 percent divorce rate, and the highly observant have a divorce rate below 5 percent."*

These findings encouraged me to learn more about their philosophy and I came across Rabbi Friedman with over 20 years of experience in marriage counselling, highly knowledgeable and he equally abandoned the conventional therapy by being unhappy with of the results.

As a professional - the most important thing for us is indeed the success rate - and these things we learn over time and the results you see. We see couple's approaches to their union - what they chose to absorb, what they chose to discard, their philosophy and weigh with their happiness levels and ultimately if they split. And that is the basis that I have been using as I adjust my form of therapy.

So another thing that I noticed - the value system. People that put their career in front of everything, that tend to be against the idea of marriage and have a strong preference for cohabitation, self-centred ideas, the "worship" of happiness and Love - this creates a toll on the relationship as they suck the energies from each other and expect happiness and love to be predominant and if not there is a lot of pressure in the relationship itself because it is very difficult to put that responsibility on another partner.

When the emotion of "Love" oscillates (which is the most normal thing ever) it bugs them too much plus lack the understanding that Love is unstable and marriage is stable.

So marrying for love alone does not appear to be a wise decision it needs to be for the person but not for what the person can give as the main goal. In other words - marry each other. Not marry the love we have for each other.

The cohabitating group that has "breaking up" as a fresh option – appear to be more prone to experience instability. On another note, the couples that have the mind-set that - "Things are going through a very chaotic period, it has been extremely difficult BUT all I know is that this is the woman/man I want to spend my life with and I cannot imagine being apart from her/him." - this speech they make and belief system allows them to approach the situation on a much wiser note, the effort levels, the security and putting family first – works greatly to their advantage in terms of success within the relationship and perceiving obstacles for what they are. You can see a huge difference when compared to the cohabitating group that does not believe in anything and rather against it.

These realisations have strongly contributed for choosing certain Rabbis because the approach we use plays the highest role for the success rate. This approach allows arranged marriages to be successful too and of course when both sides share the same values and mind-set.

When that is not present - the unsettledness, the lack of feeling appreciated, the expectations and pressure is never ending – but all of this can be fixed by taking a look at our value system and adjust it accordingly.

For a human being – doubt is the worst thing ever and highly responsible for unsettledness – so much so that we even make up ideas and interpretations in our minds when we lack understanding of the situations.

One interesting experiment was, they put a few stones and divided by two colours. One of the colours when the person touches it they got hurt, and the other colour the person had a 50% chance of getting hurt or not. The ones they touched and knew they would get hurt, they did not bother when they touched it - even though it was a negative feeling. The other colour that they were uncertain regarding the outcome they would show signs of anxiety before touching it. This experiment shows that even if we know that the outcome is undesirable it is still more comfortable and better than doubt. Regardless if there is a chance of being something good. So eliminating doubt is also an important factor.

Life is uncertain and we cannot predict things. But factors such as values, moral code, decisions – this is not determined by circumstances going up or down. The secret is to carry our values regardless of how difficult life gets, and this is the certainty that when it is not present in a relationship leads to a lot of instability and negative feelings.

Regardless of the circumstances your kids will ALWAYS REMAIN your kids, your parents and siblings. As a spouse – this is the certainty that brings security in the relationship.

By holding these values – the person will always be important regardless of the circumstances or the feelings that oscillate.

There are things in life that are unchangeable. Even when a close family member passes on – the relationship and the degree of importance maintains. For as much as one can love their cat the cat will never be more important than their kid for example.

A spouse, on the other hand is the strongest connection between two people, because they become one flesh and therefore cannot live without one another. That's why the tendency is always to miss each other regardless of the circumstances but you may find that when it comes to other forms of relationship one can do without seeing one another for a larger period of time.

CHAPTER 8

A Life with a Purpose

What is your purpose in life?

How does one bring meaning to life?

Do you look forward for the day ahead of you?

When your day is over and you reflect upon it, do you feel content about how you chose to spend your day?

We all exceptionally unique, we have been given completely different gifts, where we were born, the culture we were born in, the things we passionate about that lightens us up when we speak about them, our struggles, battles, strengths, taste of things, tendencies – all of these things were not acquired by free choice but rather happened on default, in other words, we were created like that.

What we all have in common and are indeed free choice is:

1) Time – we have all be given 24 hours a day

2) We choose how to use the 24h hours

3) Our moral code – we choose how to act, love or hate, tolerant or intolerant, honest or dishonest, kind or hate speech and so forth...

One of the main characteristics that we have in relations to animas is that we tend to aspire to be more than what we are. Animals are usually content with their nature – an ant does not wish to be a bear.

In general a human-being is not content with oneself and there is a constant desire to be more. This equally comes hand in hand with our intelligence and reasoning that basically allowed us to rule over any other creature on earth.

I always like to hear people's views regarding their own mortality and the different age groups. I found that the majority of people that feel that they are not needed – tend to wake up to nothing, no purpose but simply experience the days as ordinary and empty – they tend to feel lifeless and therefore do not mind dying at any point.

I equally noticed that people get frustrated when they feel that they are NOT making an impact on earth – it can easily cause depression and demotivation too – although, they cannot pin point why they feel dead inside nor do they know how to change the situation.

So, why did mention about passions, tastes, strengths, gifts, place of birth, battles – not being free choice and each of us being unique?

Because we need to stop looking at things from a narrow perspective but rather the big picture. I am certain that a handful of people may have realized that what once looked like a curse and may have led to suffering when you look back it turned out to be a blessing.

I am equally aware that many of you have also realized that the cycle of life is perfectly made and whenever men tries to interfere with the smallest thing – it disrupts the cycle – absolutely always! So I equally hope that men had realised that he does not have control over nature and a magnitude of things – the degree of intelligence in nature is mind blowing.

This is to say that ALL creations have their purpose whether we want to classify them as good or bad – they are essential.

To try and illustrate this conclusion: Each of us are a piece of a huge and complex puzzle that we have not been able to understand it as a whole and probably never will – theories have been developed but theories are not facts but rather hypothesis.

So, this is my suggestion:

1) What battles and weaknesses that were installed in you as default?

What if I told you that the entire purpose is so that you may learn to effectively overcome it? Why are you supposed to overcome this? – This you know best, dig in.

2) What are the gifts, strengths and passions that were installed in you as default?

This is what you should be focusing on heavily. Be the BEST as you can be and excel in your gifts, you will be amazed by what you can become and do not compare yourself with anyone else – their path is theirs and unique too. Each path is essential.

3) Your place of birth and all?

How does this correlate with the abovementioned conclusions?

4) What is your purpose?

Take a look around you and identify who needs you? What do they need you for? How can you effectively serve others and bring a contribution and change in those around you? This goes in phases and it's a process, it starts from the ones close to you, the community, and your country ... the world.

Do not go for monetary gains, do not go for economy, do not go for success – all these motives will not take you there. As those things do not give meaning to one's life. Do it from your heart, give your very best and success naturally follows as a consequence.

I will never say that it is easy, the obstacles and failures are inevitable but each of them comes with great wisdom so they are essential. There is no effective learning without failure. People will demotivate you but you do not need absolutely anyone to believe in you except yourself – That is the only requirement.

What I can promise you right now is that it is worth it. The feeling of accomplishment, of putting a smile on someone else's face, of making a difference, of making a contribution to the world –

This is what we call purpose.

As you see above – many times we think that happiness is when we have certain things working the way we want to. Look back and realize the things you have once dreamed of and you have them today – if they do not give you a sense of fulfilment you are probably looking at the wrong direction, do not place all your focus on acquiring more and more of it as you shall not feel very different from what you feel right now. This frame of thinking is what leads to destination addiction – you never get there.

We as human-beings are not wired that way – we want to feel needed. So – if you are not happy about certain things and you wish they were different do not run away from it. Your purpose is to make that change you want to see.

Do not get discouraged, do not feel hopeless.

Be the change you want to see in the world.

Each act we make has an effect. There is no such thing as small or big act – there are acts.

My prayer to you, reading this book is that you find meaning in your life, purpose and that you excel and shine with the gift God has given to you. Amen

Conclusion

This book is relevant for psychology students and any individual who wish to learn and benefit from expert knowledge on the field of Psychology. I found that a great amount of information is not easily available and therefore I chose to share with you the most wonderful gift that holds the potential of empowering any individual – Wisdom.

Wisdom allows us to perceive life in a more profound way, finding meaning in our experiences and understand that everything in life is seasonal. It allows us to understand the storms and use them to get stronger and fly higher above like the eagles do. It allows us to see the unseen, go to places no one else has ever been, experience things in a more profound manner and allows us develop high levels of empathy.

In order to illustrate the depth of wisdom, I shall refer to when Jesus Christ was at the cross, after being tortured and humiliated, he turn to his Father in Heaven and said: ''Father, please forgive them as they do not know what they are doing.''

Acknowledgements

I would like show infinite gratitude to God, The Holy one who is my Father in Heaven. I would like to thank him deeply for every experience and exposure I went through thoughout my journey in life that allowed me to accumulate so much wisdom. I thank him for providing me with the gift of communication, connect with people and the passion for writing as it allows me to share the message.

I am his servant and pray that he guides me into revealing the truth and ensure that I always share the Truth.

I would like to thank my parents Selma Ismael Sema and Roodolf Raston for the endless sacrifices they have done for me, for believing in me and being absolutely amazing, encouraging and caring at all times.

I would like to thank all the wonderful people that had crossed my path, that have given me unconditional support, love, kindness – who have had a great contribution to my growth – you know who you are.

With Love,

Sharlene Sema Raston